Beef up your revision muscles with CGP!

It's not easy to rack up a high score in GCSE PE — and the new
Grade 9-1 course is tougher than ever. Luckily, help is at hand...

This brilliant CGP Revision Guide explains every key topic you'll need to understand
for the exams, from dorsi-flexion to data analysis! There are also plenty of
exam-style questions to test you on what you've learned.

We've also included advice on how to pick up as many marks as possible,
so you'll be ready to tackle your exams and finish with style.

CGP — still the best! ☺

Our sole aim here at CGP is to produce the highest quality books —
carefully written, immaculately presented and dangerously close to being funny.

Then we work our socks off to get them out to you
— at the cheapest possible prices.

Contents

Section Five — Sport Psychology

Section Six — Sport, Society and Culture

Section Seven — Using Data

Published by CGP

Editors:
Chris Corrall, Joanna Daniels and Alison Palin.

Contributor:
Paddy Gannon

With thanks to Chris Cope and Glenn Rogers for the proofreading.

With thanks to Ana Pungartnik for the copyright research.

Definitions from Edexcel specifications used with the permission of Pearson Education.

Definition of health on page 22 is from the preamble to the Constitution of the World Health Organization, as adopted by the International Health Conference, New York, 19 June - 22 July 1946; signed on 22 July 1946 by the representatives of 61 States (Official Records of the World Health Organization, no. 2, p.100), and entered into force on 7 April 1948.

Normative data table for grip dynamometer test on page 31 was published in 'Physical Education and the Study of Sport' 4th ed, 2002, Davis ed, p.123, 1 table ('Normative data table for grip strength test' for 16 to 19 year olds), Copyright Elsevier (2016).

Normative data for 35 m sprint test on page 31 from ARKINSTALL, M et al. (2010) VCE Physical Education 2. Malaysia: Macmillan. p.250. © Reproduced by permission of Macmillan Education Australia.

Data about obesity rates on page 48 copyright © 2015, Health and Social Care Information Centre. All rights reserved.

Graph of participation rates in sports on page 66 based on data from Sport England.

Source for data about shirt sponsorship in the Premier League on page 68: sportingintelligence.com.

ISBN: 978 1 78294 532 1
Printed by Elanders Ltd, Newcastle upon Tyne.
Clipart from Corel®

The Skeletal System

Welcome to the GCSE PE fun bus — first stop is the <u>skeleton</u>. It gives the body its <u>shape</u> and has loads of <u>jobs</u> to do. It's made up of various kinds of <u>bones</u>, all with their own function. Here we go...

The Skeleton has Different Functions

The skeleton does <u>more</u> than you might think to help your performance in sport. Its main functions are:

① <u>SUPPORT/SHAPE</u>:

1) The skeleton is a <u>rigid bone frame</u> for the rest of the body. Our <u>shape</u> is mainly due to our <u>skeleton</u>.

2) The skeleton <u>supports</u> the <u>soft tissues</u> like skin and muscle.

3) This helps you to have good <u>posture</u>, which is <u>essential</u> in loads of sports.

4) E.g. good posture aids <u>performance</u> in <u>gymnastics</u>.

③ <u>MOVEMENT</u>:

1) <u>Muscles</u>, <u>attached</u> to bones by <u>tendons</u>, can <u>move</u> bones at <u>joints</u>.

2) This movement is essential for good <u>performance</u> in sport.

3) There are different <u>types of movement</u> at the various <u>joints</u>, which are important in <u>different sports</u>.

② <u>PROTECTION</u>:

1) Bones are very <u>tough</u> — they <u>protect vital organs</u> like the <u>brain</u>, <u>heart</u> and <u>lungs</u>.

2) This allows you to <u>perform well</u> in sport without fear of serious <u>injury</u>.

3) E.g. the <u>skull</u> protects the brain, so you can <u>head</u> a football or take punches in a boxing match <u>without serious injury</u>.

④ <u>MAKING BLOOD CELLS/PLATELETS</u>:

1) Some <u>bones</u> contain <u>bone marrow</u>, which makes the components of <u>blood</u> — <u>platelets</u> and red and white <u>blood cells</u> (see p9).

2) <u>Red blood cells</u> are really <u>important</u> during exercise — they transport the <u>oxygen</u> that muscles need to move.

3) Athletes with <u>more</u> red blood cells <u>perform better</u> — <u>more oxygen</u> can be delivered to their muscles.

⑤ <u>MINERAL STORAGE</u>:

1) Bones store <u>minerals</u> like <u>calcium</u> and <u>phosphorus</u>.

2) These help with <u>bone strength</u> — so you're less likely to <u>break</u> a bone.

3) They're also needed for <u>muscle contraction</u> — so the body can <u>move</u>.

There are Different Types of Bone in the Skeleton

There are <u>four</u> main types of bone in the skeleton. Each type is <u>suited</u> to a different <u>purpose</u>.

Long Bones

Long bones (e.g. the humerus in the arm) are <u>strong</u> and are used by muscles to assist <u>movement</u>.

Short Bones

Short bones (e.g. the tarsals in the foot) <u>support</u> the weight of the body — they're <u>weight-bearing</u>.

<u>Short</u> bones are also used in some smaller <u>fine movements</u>, e.g. moving the hand at the wrist. <u>Long</u> bones are used for larger <u>gross movements</u>, e.g. moving the leg at the hip (see p56).

Irregular Bones

Irregular bones (e.g. the vertebrae of the spine) are suited to <u>protection</u> and <u>muscle</u> attachment.

Flat Bones

Flat bones (e.g. the ribs) <u>protect</u> internal organs. Their broad surface also allows <u>muscle attachment</u>.

Have no fear — I'll protect you.

Aw, thanks.

I bet you found that all extremely humerus...

It's really important that you remember all the different functions of the skeleton, and how each one helps your performance in physical activity and sport. Have a go at this Exam Practice Question to test your knowledge.

Q1 Explain **one** way that the skeleton's mineral storage function aids performance in physical activity and sport.

[2 marks]

The Skeletal System

Time for some more skeleton-related fun — this page'll give you a hand at remembering the <u>names</u> of some <u>important bones</u> in the body, their types and <u>what they do</u>. I bet you can hardly wait...

Learn the Structure of the Skeleton

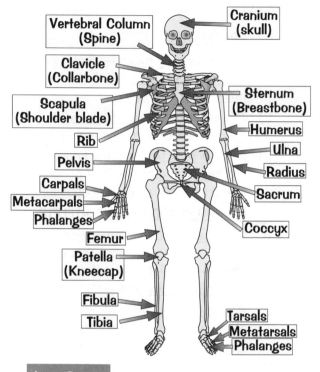

Vertebral Column (Spine)
Cranium (skull)
Clavicle (Collarbone)
Scapula (Shoulder blade)
Sternum (Breastbone)
Rib
Humerus
Pelvis
Ulna
Carpals
Radius
Metacarpals
Sacrum
Phalanges
Femur
Coccyx
Patella (Kneecap)
Fibula
Tibia
Tarsals
Metatarsals
Phalanges

Flat Bones

<u>Cranium</u> — <u>protects</u> the brain.

<u>Sternum</u> and <u>ribs</u> — <u>protect</u> the heart and lungs. The ribs also protect the kidneys.

<u>Scapula</u> — <u>protects</u> the shoulder joint and has many <u>muscles</u> attached to it, helping arm and shoulder <u>movement</u>.

<u>Pelvis</u> — <u>protects</u> the reproductive organs and the bladder. It also has many muscles attached to it, helping leg <u>movement</u>.

Short Bones

<u>Carpals</u> — form the <u>wrist</u> and give it <u>stability</u>, allowing <u>movement</u> of the hand.

<u>Tarsals</u> — bear the body's <u>weight</u> when on foot, e.g. during standing and running.

<u>The patella</u> is a different type of bone — it's a <u>sesamoid bone</u>. It protects the <u>tendon</u> that crosses the knee joint by stopping it <u>rubbing</u> against the femur.

Long Bones

<u>Clavicle</u> — forms part of the <u>shoulder joint</u> to assist arm <u>movement</u>.

<u>Humerus</u> — used by muscles to <u>move</u> the <u>whole</u> arm, e.g. swinging a badminton racket.

<u>Ulna</u> and <u>radius</u> — used by muscles to <u>move</u> the lower arm, e.g. bending at the elbow.

<u>Femur</u> — used by muscles to <u>move</u> the <u>whole</u> leg, e.g. when running.

<u>Fibula</u> and <u>tibia</u> — used by muscles to <u>move</u> the lower leg, e.g. to kick a football.

<u>Metacarpals</u> — used by muscles to allow the hand to <u>grip</u>, e.g. to hold a cricket ball.

<u>Phalanges</u> — used by muscles to <u>move</u> and <u>bend</u> the fingers and toes.

<u>Metatarsals</u> — used by muscles to <u>move</u> the foot, e.g. when jumping.

Learn the Structure of the Vertebral Column

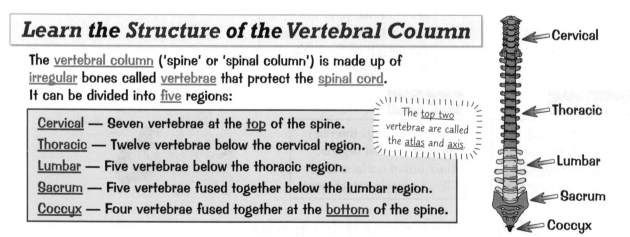

The <u>vertebral column</u> ('spine' or 'spinal column') is made up of <u>irregular</u> bones called <u>vertebrae</u> that protect the <u>spinal cord</u>. It can be divided into <u>five</u> regions:

Cervical

The <u>top two</u> vertebrae are called the <u>atlas</u> and <u>axis</u>.

Thoracic

Lumbar

Sacrum

Coccyx

<u>Cervical</u> — Seven vertebrae at the <u>top</u> of the spine.

<u>Thoracic</u> — Twelve vertebrae below the cervical region.

<u>Lumbar</u> — Five vertebrae below the thoracic region.

<u>Sacrum</u> — Five vertebrae fused together below the lumbar region.

<u>Coccyx</u> — Four vertebrae fused together at the <u>bottom</u> of the spine.

Now, use your phalanges to pick up a pen and paper...

Now you know all about the skeleton's structure, give this Exam Practice Question a go.

Q1 Name the **two** bones of the lower leg. [2 marks]

The Skeletal System

Joints are really important parts of the skeleton — you need to know what they are, how they can move and what types of joints you'll find in the body. Luckily, all that is right here on this page.

There are Different Kinds of Joint Movement

1) Joints are any points where two or more bones meet. The bones that meet at a joint are called the articulating bones of the joint.

2) Here are a few examples of some of the major joints in the body, and their articulating bones:

3) There are eight joint movements that you need to know:

Hip — pelvis and femur

Shoulder — humerus and scapula

Knee — femur and tibia

Ankle — tibia, fibula and talus (one of the tarsals)

Elbow — humerus, radius and ulna

FLEXION

Closing a joint, e.g. the wrist movement during a basketball throw.

EXTENSION

Opening a joint, e.g. kicking a football.

ADDUCTION

Moving towards an imaginary centre line, e.g. swinging a golf club.

ABDUCTION
Moving away from an imaginary centre line, e.g. taking back a tennis racket before swinging it.

ROTATION
Clockwise or anticlockwise movement, e.g. the leg movement during a turnout in ballet.

CIRCUMDUCTION

Movement of a limb, hand or foot in a circular motion, e.g. to bowl a cricket ball.

PLANTAR-FLEXION

Extension at the ankle, e.g. pointing the toes during gymnastics.

DORSI-FLEXION

Flexion at the ankle, e.g. lifting the toes during gymnastics.

You might see this called 'overarm rotation'.

There are different Joint Types in the Body

You need to know about ball and socket, pivot, hinge and condyloid joints. Each type allows a certain range of movements.

type	examples	flexion and extension	adduction and abduction	rotation	circumduction
ball and socket	hip, shoulder	✓	✓	✓	✓
hinge	knee, ankle, elbow	✓	✗	✗	✗
condyloid	wrist	✓	✓	✗	✓
pivot	neck (atlas and axis)	✗	✗	✓	✗

Two bones meet at a joint — they have an excellent time together...

Make sure you learn all these joint and movement types for your exam. Now have a go at this Practice Question...

Q1 State the joint type that allows the widest range of movement types. [1 mark]

The Skeletal System

Coming up on this page — a little more on joint movements, as well as what joints are made of.
Spoiler alert — they're made of more than just bones. Sorry to ruin the surprise of it all...

Sports use lots of different Movement Types

During exercise, you'll usually use a combination of movement types, and often a combination of joints, either at the same time, or one after another. For example:

1) To do a push-up at the gym or a football throw-in, first you use flexion at the elbow to bend your arms. To straighten your arms again and complete the movements, you extend your arms at the elbow.

2) Running, kicking, basic squats and standing vertical jumps all use flexion and extension at the hip and knee. They also use plantar-flexion and dorsi-flexion at the ankle.

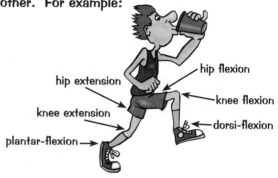

hip flexion
knee flexion
dorsi-flexion
hip extension
knee extension
plantar-flexion

Connective Tissues Join Muscle and Bones

There are three types of connective tissue you need to know about:

LIGAMENTS — hold bones together to restrict how much joints can move. This helps maintain the stability of the skeleton and prevents dislocation of joints (see p41). They're made of tough and fibrous tissue (like very strong string).

Ligaments also protect bones and joints by absorbing shock.

TENDONS — attach muscles to bones (or to other muscles) to allow bones to move when muscles contract.

CARTILAGE — acts as a cushion between bones to prevent damage during joint movement.

Learn the Structure of a Synovial Joint

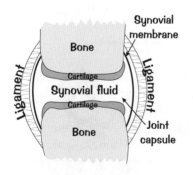

Synovial membrane
Bone
Ligament
Cartilage
Synovial fluid
Cartilage
Bone
Ligament
Joint capsule

Ball and socket, hinge, condyloid and pivot joints are all synovial joints. A synovial joint is a joint that allows a wide range of movement and has a joint capsule enclosing and supporting it.

1) The bones at a synovial joint are held together by ligaments.

2) The ends of the bones are covered with cartilage and are shaped so that they fit together and can move smoothly.

3) The synovial membrane releases synovial fluid into the joint capsule to lubricate (or 'oil') the joint, allowing it to move more easily.

4) Most synovial joints also have sacs of fluid called bursae (one is a 'bursa') which reduce friction between bones and tissues in and around the joint.

5) This structure helps to prevent injury to the bones that make up your joints.

All this talk about joints is making me really hungry...

Those connective tissues are really important — they all help your performance in physical activity and sport in a different way. Here are another couple of Exam Practice Questions on joints for you to have a go at.

Q1 Analyse the movement that occurs at the elbow joint during a pass in netball. [2 marks]

Q2 Explain the impact of cartilage on performance in physical activity and sport. [3 marks]

The Muscular System

The <u>skeletal system</u> can't make the body move <u>on its own</u> — it needs some help from the <u>muscular system</u>. Together, they're known as the <u>musculo-skeletal system</u>.

There are Different Types of Muscle

1) Like the title says, there are <u>different types of muscle</u> you need to know about. These are...

VOLUNTARY (SKELETAL) MUSCLES
Attached to the <u>skeleton</u> and are under <u>your control</u>. They help to <u>move</u> the body.

INVOLUNTARY (SMOOTH) MUSCLES
Work internal organs <u>without effort</u> from you, e.g. muscles in <u>blood vessels</u> control the amount of blood flowing to <u>voluntary muscles</u>.

2) <u>Cardiac</u> muscle is a type of <u>involuntary</u> muscle that forms the <u>heart</u>.

3) It <u>never</u> gets tired — the heart can pump blood around your body <u>all the time</u>.

4) During <u>exercise</u>, <u>voluntary</u> muscles need <u>oxygen</u> so they can <u>move</u> the body. When the heart beats, it <u>pumps blood</u> carrying oxygen to these muscles.

Each Muscle has a Specific Function

You need to learn the <u>names</u> of some <u>voluntary muscles</u>, and what their <u>main functions</u> are.

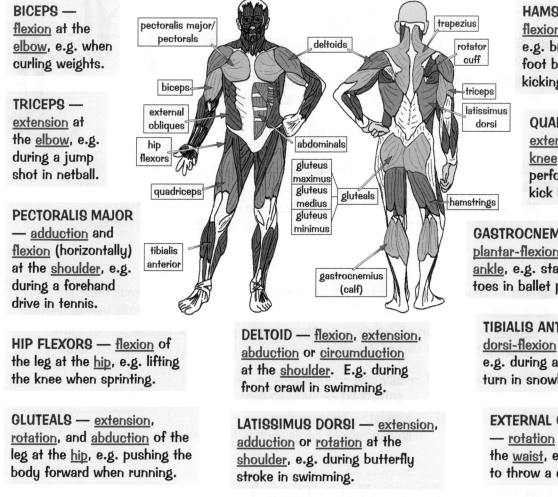

BICEPS — <u>flexion</u> at the <u>elbow</u>, e.g. when curling weights.

TRICEPS — <u>extension</u> at the <u>elbow</u>, e.g. during a jump shot in netball.

PECTORALIS MAJOR — <u>adduction</u> and <u>flexion</u> (horizontally) at the <u>shoulder</u>, e.g. during a forehand drive in tennis.

HIP FLEXORS — <u>flexion</u> of the leg at the <u>hip</u>, e.g. lifting the knee when sprinting.

GLUTEALS — <u>extension</u>, <u>rotation</u>, and <u>abduction</u> of the leg at the <u>hip</u>, e.g. pushing the body forward when running.

TRAPEZIUS — <u>extension</u> at the <u>neck</u> (tilting the head back), e.g. preparing to head a football.

DELTOID — <u>flexion</u>, <u>extension</u>, <u>abduction</u> or <u>circumduction</u> at the <u>shoulder</u>. E.g. during front crawl in swimming.

LATISSIMUS DORSI — <u>extension</u>, <u>adduction</u> or <u>rotation</u> at the <u>shoulder</u>, e.g. during butterfly stroke in swimming.

ROTATOR CUFFS — <u>rotation</u> and <u>abduction</u> at the <u>shoulder</u>, e.g. lifting the arms when preparing to dive. They also <u>stabilise</u> the shoulder joint during other movements.

HAMSTRINGS — <u>flexion</u> at the <u>knee</u>, e.g. bringing the foot back before kicking a football.

QUADRICEPS — <u>extension</u> at the <u>knee</u>, e.g. when performing a drop kick in rugby.

GASTROCNEMIUS — <u>plantar-flexion</u> at the <u>ankle</u>, e.g. standing on the toes in ballet pointe work.

TIBIALIS ANTERIOR — <u>dorsi-flexion</u> at the <u>ankle</u>, e.g. during a heel side turn in snowboarding.

EXTERNAL OBLIQUES — <u>rotation</u> or <u>flexion</u> at the <u>waist</u>, e.g. preparing to throw a discus.

ABDOMINALS — <u>flexion</u> at the <u>waist</u>, e.g. during a sit-up.

The Muscular System

Now on to more stuff about muscles — just what we were all hoping for. This page'll look at
how muscles <u>work together</u> to produce different movement types at the <u>joints</u> in the body.

Antagonistic Muscles Work in Pairs

Muscles can only do one thing — <u>pull</u>. To make a joint move in two directions,
you need <u>two muscles</u> that can pull in <u>opposite directions</u>.

1) <u>Antagonistic</u> muscles are <u>pairs of muscles</u> that work <u>against</u> each other.
2) One muscle <u>contracts</u> while the other one <u>relaxes</u>, and <u>vice versa</u>.
3) The muscle that's contracting is the <u>agonist</u> or <u>prime mover</u>.
4) The muscle that's relaxing is the <u>antagonist</u>.
5) Each muscle is attached to <u>two</u> bones by <u>tendons</u>.
6) Only <u>one</u> of the bones connected at the joint actually moves.

Here, 'contracts' means 'shortens', and 'relaxes' means 'lengthens'. But you might see 'contracts' used to mean 'creates tension' — which muscles do when they shorten and lengthen (see next page).

During this antagonistic muscle action, other muscles can <u>help</u> the agonist to work properly by
<u>stabilising</u> it where it attaches to the bone that doesn't move. These muscles are known as <u>fixators</u>.

You need to know some Antagonistic Muscle Pairs

There are <u>antagonistic muscle pairs</u> at different <u>joints</u> in the body:

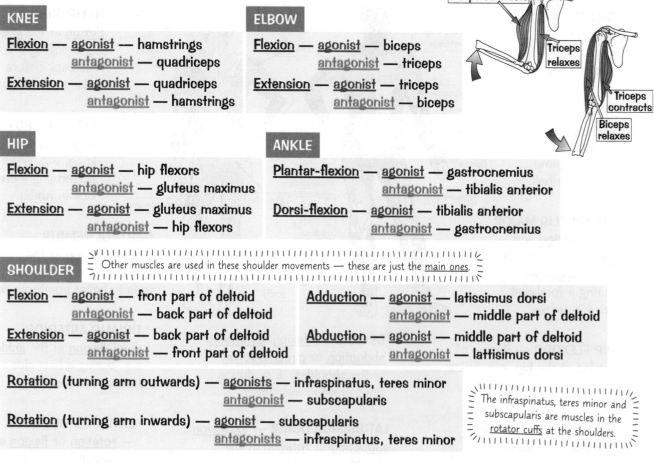

KNEE

<u>Flexion</u> — <u>agonist</u> — hamstrings
<u>antagonist</u> — quadriceps
<u>Extension</u> — <u>agonist</u> — quadriceps
<u>antagonist</u> — hamstrings

ELBOW

<u>Flexion</u> — <u>agonist</u> — biceps
<u>antagonist</u> — triceps
<u>Extension</u> — <u>agonist</u> — triceps
<u>antagonist</u> — biceps

HIP

<u>Flexion</u> — <u>agonist</u> — hip flexors
<u>antagonist</u> — gluteus maximus
<u>Extension</u> — <u>agonist</u> — gluteus maximus
<u>antagonist</u> — hip flexors

ANKLE

<u>Plantar-flexion</u> — <u>agonist</u> — gastrocnemius
<u>antagonist</u> — tibialis anterior
<u>Dorsi-flexion</u> — <u>agonist</u> — tibialis anterior
<u>antagonist</u> — gastrocnemius

SHOULDER

Other muscles are used in these shoulder movements — these are just the main ones.

<u>Flexion</u> — <u>agonist</u> — front part of deltoid
<u>antagonist</u> — back part of deltoid
<u>Extension</u> — <u>agonist</u> — back part of deltoid
<u>antagonist</u> — front part of deltoid

<u>Adduction</u> — <u>agonist</u> — latissimus dorsi
<u>antagonist</u> — middle part of deltoid
<u>Abduction</u> — <u>agonist</u> — middle part of deltoid
<u>antagonist</u> — lattisimus dorsi

<u>Rotation</u> (turning arm outwards) — <u>agonists</u> — infraspinatus, teres minor
<u>antagonist</u> — subscapularis
<u>Rotation</u> (turning arm inwards) — <u>agonist</u> — subscapularis
<u>antagonists</u> — infraspinatus, teres minor

The infraspinatus, teres minor and subscapularis are muscles in the <u>rotator cuffs</u> at the shoulders.

Is that a bacon rope I see? Nope, it's a hamstring...

This 'antagonistic muscle pair' stuff might seem a bit tricky, but just remember — the muscle that's the agonist in
one movement will be the antagonist in the opposite movement. Here's an Exam Practice Question for you to try.

Q1 State the agonist muscle group that works to produce the hip
movement when bringing the leg forward to kick a football.

[1 mark]

The Muscular System

Hooray — you've reached the third and final page about the muscular system. It's all about <u>how muscles contract</u> and the different types of <u>fibres</u> that make up the muscles in your body.

There are Different Types of Muscle Contraction

You don't need this bit if you're doing the <u>Edexcel</u> or <u>OCR</u> course.

When a muscle <u>contracts</u>, it creates <u>tension</u> to <u>apply force</u> to a bone. Muscle contractions can be <u>isometric</u> or <u>isotonic</u>.

ISOMETRIC CONTRACTION
The muscle <u>stays the same length</u>, and so nothing moves.

Like if you pull on a rope attached to a wall.

ISOTONIC CONTRACTION
The muscle <u>changes length</u> and so something moves.

Like if you exercise with weights that are free to move.

There are also <u>two types</u> of <u>isotonic</u> contraction — <u>concentric</u> and <u>eccentric</u>.

CONCENTRIC CONTRACTION
This is when a muscle contracts and <u>shortens</u>. This type of contraction <u>pulls</u> on a bone to cause a <u>movement</u> to happen. E.g. during the <u>upward</u> phase of a <u>biceps curl</u>, your <u>biceps</u> undergoes a concentric contraction to <u>pull</u> your forearm and <u>lift</u> the weight.

ECCENTRIC CONTRACTION
This is when a muscle contracts and <u>lengthens</u>. This helps you to <u>control</u> the <u>speed</u> of a movement. E.g. during the <u>downward</u> phase of a <u>biceps curl</u>, your <u>biceps</u> contracts eccentrically, creating <u>tension</u> so that the weight falls <u>slowly</u>.

Different Types of Muscle Fibre suit Different Activities

1) All <u>muscles</u> are made up of <u>fibres</u>.
2) These muscle fibres can be <u>slow twitch</u> (type I) or <u>fast twitch</u> (type IIA and type IIX).

If you're doing the <u>AQA</u> course, you can skip this part of the page.

SLOW TWITCH

<u>TYPE I</u> — Suited to <u>low intensity aerobic</u> work (e.g. marathon running) as they can be used for a <u>long</u> period of time without fatiguing.

See p13 for the definitions of aerobic and anaerobic work.

FAST TWITCH

<u>TYPE IIA</u> — Used in <u>anaerobic</u> work, but can be <u>improved</u> through <u>endurance training</u> to increase their resistance to fatigue.

<u>TYPE IIX</u> — Used in <u>anaerobic</u> work. Can generate a much greater <u>force</u> than other fibre types but <u>fatigue</u> quickly. Useful in short bursts of exercise, e.g. a <u>100 m sprint</u>.

Sheila was chuffed that she'd found a use for her type I muscle fibres.

Eccentric muscle contractions — not just by strange muscles...

Lots of definitions on this page, so make sure you learn the ones you need for your exam. Try these Practice Questions next — the first one is about the top half of this page, and the second one is about the bottom half.

Q1   State the muscle group that performs an eccentric contraction at the knee during the lowering phase of a squat.   [1 mark]

Q2   Which one of the following muscle fibre types is best suited for use in a long distance triathlon?

    A Type I   **B** Type IIA   **C** Type IIX   **D** Fast twitch   [1 mark]

The Cardiovascular System

Your cardiovascular system's job is to move blood around your body. As the blood travels around, it does loads of really useful stuff to help you take part in physical activity and sport. Read on to find out more...

The Cardiovascular System has Three Main Functions

TRANSPORT OF SUBSTANCES — Transporting things around the body in the bloodstream, like oxygen, carbon dioxide, and nutrients (e.g. glucose). This gives the muscles what they need to release energy to move during exercise (and takes away any waste products).

Have a look at p13 for more about how muscles use oxygen and glucose.

TEMPERATURE CONTROL — Moving more blood nearer the skin cools the body more quickly. This means you can exercise for a long time without overheating.

CLOTTING OF WOUNDS — Your blood clots to seal cuts. This stops you bleeding too much if you get a cut, and helps to prevent wounds becoming infected.

Learn How the Heart Pumps Blood Around the Body

1) The cardiovascular system is made up of three main parts — the heart, blood and blood vessels.

Arteries, veins and capillaries are the main types of blood vessel.

2) During any kind of physical activity, blood needs to circulate around the body to deliver oxygen and glucose to your muscles, and to take carbon dioxide away from them.

3) The cardiovascular system has a double-circulatory system — this just means there are two circuits:

PULMONARY CIRCUIT

Pressure in the heart causes the valves to open. They close to stop blood flowing the wrong way.

- Deoxygenated blood enters the right ventricle through the tricuspid valve.
- The right ventricle contracts, pushing the blood through the right semi-lunar valve into the pulmonary artery, which carries the blood to the lungs to be oxygenated.
- Oxygenated blood from the lungs enters the left atrium through the pulmonary veins.

The word for more than one atrium is 'atria'.

SYSTEMIC CIRCUIT

- Oxygenated blood enters the left ventricle through the bicuspid valve.
- The left ventricle contracts, pushing the blood through the left semi-lunar valve into the aorta (an artery), which carries the oxygenated blood to the rest of the body — including the muscles.
- When the muscles have used the oxygen in the blood, it becomes deoxygenated. It then enters the right atrium through the vena cava vein.

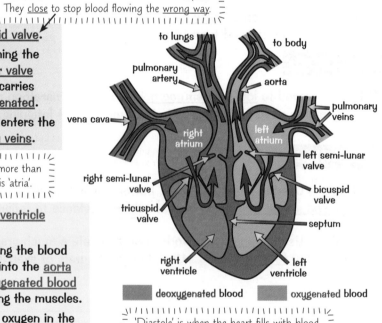

to lungs · to body · pulmonary artery · aorta · pulmonary veins · vena cava · right atrium · left atrium · left semi-lunar valve · right semi-lunar valve · bicuspid valve · tricuspid valve · septum · right ventricle · left ventricle

deoxygenated blood   oxygenated blood

'Diastole' is when the heart fills with blood. 'Systole' is when it pumps the blood out.

The heart — it's all just pump and circumstance...

The 'left's and 'right's on the heart diagram mean on the person whose heart it is — that's why they're reversed. Now, get learning what all the bits of the cardiovascular system do, and try this Practice Question.

Q1 Analyse the role of the pulmonary artery in physical activity and sport. [4 marks]

The Cardiovascular System

Your cardiovascular system has different types of blood vessels that carry blood around your body.
This page'll tell you all about them, as well as all the weird and wonderful stuff your blood is made of.

Arteries, Veins and Capillaries Carry Blood

1) Blood vessels transport blood — they have a hollow centre called the lumen so blood can flow through.

2) Different types of blood vessel are suited to different roles:

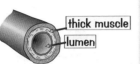

thick muscle
lumen

ARTERIES — carry blood away from the heart. All arteries carry oxygenated blood except for the pulmonary arteries. Their thick, muscular walls allow them to carry blood flowing at high pressure.

Blood pressure is how strongly the blood presses against the walls of blood vessels.

The (smooth) muscle in the walls of arteries and veins allows them to widen and narrow to control blood flow (see p15).

large lumen
thin muscle
thin wall

VEINS — carry blood towards the heart. They have valves to stop blood flowing the wrong way. All veins carry deoxygenated blood, except for the pulmonary veins. They carry blood at low pressure, so they have thinner walls and less muscle than arteries.

thin wall

CAPILLARIES — carry blood through the body to exchange gases and nutrients with the body's tissues. They have very thin walls so substances can easily pass through. They're also very narrow, which means lots of them can fit into the body's tissues — giving them a large surface area to let gas exchange happen more easily. It also means that blood can only flow through them slowly — giving more time for gas exchange.

Blood from arteriole — tissue — Blood to venule — capillaries

3) There are also two other small types of blood vessel — arterioles (which branch off arteries) and venules (which meet to form veins).

4) Oxygenated blood flows through arteries into arterioles, then into capillaries.

5) After gases have been exchanged between the capillaries and the body tissues, blood is transported from the capillaries into venules, where it flows back into the veins.

Your Blood is made up of Cells, Platelets and Plasma

Lots of different things make up the blood in your body. Each bit has its own job, which is really important in helping your body to take part in physical activity.

RED BLOOD CELLS — Carry oxygen and transport it around the body to be used to release energy needed by muscles during physical activity. They also carry carbon dioxide to the lungs. Haemoglobin (a protein in red blood cells) stores the oxygen and carbon dioxide.

Oxyhaemoglobin is formed by oxygen and haemoglobin combining.

WHITE BLOOD CELLS — Fight against disease so you stay healthy and perform well.

PLATELETS — Help blood to clot at wounds so they don't become infected and so you don't lose too much blood.

PLASMA — carries everything in the bloodstream. That includes blood cells, digested food (e.g. glucose) and waste (e.g. carbon dioxide).

What do you call a baby dinner plate — a platelet...

Hahaha... If you're struggling to remember whether veins and arteries carry blood to or from the heart, just remember — arteries carry blood away from the heart. Here's a Practice Question for you to have a go at.

Q1 State **one** characteristic of capillaries and explain how it aids performance in physical activity and sport.

[3 marks]

The Respiratory System

You'll probably recognise most of this stuff from <u>biology</u> — but there's no harm in a <u>quick recap</u>.

Learn the Structure of the Respiratory System

The respiratory system is <u>everything</u> you use to <u>breathe</u>.
It's found in the <u>chest cavity</u> — the area inside the chest.

TRACHEA
↓
BRONCHI
↓
BRONCHIOLES
↓
ALVEOLI

1) Air passes through the nose or mouth and then on to the <u>trachea</u>.

2) The trachea splits into two tubes called <u>bronchi</u> (each one is a '<u>bronchus</u>') — one going to each <u>lung</u>.

3) The bronchi split into progressively smaller tubes called <u>bronchioles</u>.

4) The bronchioles finally end at small bags called <u>alveoli</u> (each one is an '<u>alveolus</u>') where <u>gases</u> are <u>exchanged</u> (see below).

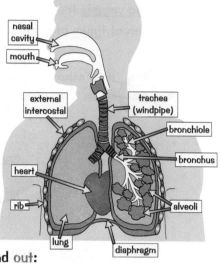

The <u>diaphragm</u> and <u>external intercostal muscles</u> help the air to move <u>in</u> and <u>out</u>:

- When you breathe <u>in</u>, the <u>diaphragm</u> and <u>external intercostals</u> contract to move the <u>ribcage</u> upwards and <u>expand</u> the chest cavity. This <u>decreases</u> the <u>air pressure</u> in the lungs, drawing air in.
- When you breathe <u>out</u>, the <u>diaphragm</u> and the <u>external intercostals</u> relax, moving the <u>ribcage</u> down and <u>shrinking</u> the chest cavity. <u>Air pressure</u> in the lungs <u>increases</u>, forcing air <u>out</u> of the lungs the <u>same way</u> it came in.

Oxygen and Carbon Dioxide are Exchanged in the Alveoli

1) The cardiovascular and respiratory systems have to <u>work together</u> to get <u>oxygen</u> to the muscles, and <u>carbon dioxide</u> away from them. They do this by <u>exchanging</u> gases between the <u>alveoli</u> and <u>capillaries</u> surrounding them.

The cardiovascular and respiratory systems together make up the <u>cardio-respiratory system</u>.

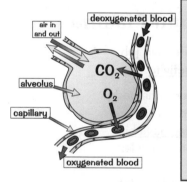

1) <u>Oxygenated blood</u> delivers <u>oxygen</u> and collects <u>carbon dioxide</u> as it <u>circulates</u> around the body. <u>Deoxygenated blood</u> returns to the <u>heart</u> and is then <u>pumped</u> to the <u>lungs</u>.

2) In the lungs, <u>carbon dioxide</u> moves from the blood in the capillaries into the <u>alveoli</u> so it can be <u>breathed out</u>.

3) <u>Oxygen</u> from the <u>air</u> you breathe into the lungs moves across from the alveoli to the <u>red blood cells</u> in the capillaries.

4) The <u>oxygenated blood</u> returns to the <u>heart</u> and is <u>pumped</u> to the rest of the body. The red blood cells <u>carry</u> the oxygen around the body and <u>deliver</u> it where it's needed, e.g. the muscles.

2) Alveoli are surrounded by lots of <u>capillaries</u>, giving them a <u>large blood supply</u> to exchange gases with.

3) They also have a <u>large surface area</u> and <u>moist</u>, <u>thin walls</u> — so gases can <u>easily</u> pass through them.

4) This <u>exchange</u> of gases happens through a process called <u>diffusion</u>. This means the gases move down a <u>concentration gradient</u> — from a place of <u>higher concentration</u> to a place of <u>lower concentration</u>:

IN ALVEOLUS		IN CAPILLARY
High concentration of O_2	DIFFUSION OF O_2 →	Low concentration of O_2
Low concentration of CO_2	← DIFFUSION OF CO_2	High concentration of CO_2

*O_2 = oxygen
CO_2 = carbon dioxide*

Air we go — keeping trachea respiratory system...

So, diffusion is pretty impressive, eh? I bet you'll be impressed with this Exam Practice Question, too.

Q1   Describe how deoxygenated blood becomes oxygenated.   [3 marks]

The Respiratory System

You might have noticed that you take <u>bigger breaths</u> when you <u>exercise</u>. That's just 'cos the air we <u>breathe in</u> contains the <u>stuff</u> we need <u>more</u> of for <u>exercise</u>, and the air we <u>breathe out</u> contains the <u>stuff we don't want</u>.

Air is made up of Different Gases

You only need to know this bit for the Edexcel course.

1) You need to know the composition of the air we <u>inhale</u> (breathe in) and <u>exhale</u> (breathe out). This just means the <u>different gases</u> it's made up of.

	% of inhaled air	% of exhaled air
Oxygen	21%	16%
Carbon dioxide	0.04%	4%
Nitrogen (as well as argon and other gases)	79%	79%

These percentages are just <u>approximate</u> values — both inhaled and exhaled air also contain small amounts of <u>water vapour</u> (exhaled air has slightly more).

2) <u>Exhaled</u> air contains <u>less oxygen</u> than inhaled air. This is because some of the <u>oxygen</u> in <u>inhaled</u> air is <u>used up</u> by the body to release <u>energy</u> through <u>aerobic respiration</u>.

3) <u>Exhaled</u> air also contains <u>more carbon dioxide</u> than inhaled air. This is because carbon dioxide is <u>produced</u> when <u>energy</u> is released through aerobic respiration. The body needs to <u>get rid</u> of this carbon dioxide, so we <u>breathe</u> it out.

Tidal Volume Increases during Exercise

1) The <u>amount of air</u> you breathe in or out during <u>one breath</u> is known as your <u>tidal volume</u>.

2) After a <u>normal breath in</u>, you can still breathe in <u>more air</u> — this extra volume of air is your <u>inspiratory reserve volume</u> (IRV).

3) You can also breathe out <u>more air</u> after a <u>normal breath out</u> — the extra air you can breathe out is your <u>expiratory reserve volume</u> (ERV).

4) During <u>exercise</u>, your <u>tidal volume</u> increases. This means your <u>IRV</u> and <u>ERV</u> decrease — you're breathing in and out <u>more air</u> than normal, so you can't breathe in or out as much <u>extra air</u>.

5) Your <u>tidal volume increases</u> for a couple of reasons:

Have a look at p13 for more about aerobic and anaerobic activity.

- To bring in <u>more oxygen</u>. This helps to release extra <u>energy</u> in the <u>muscles</u> (during <u>aerobic</u> activity) and remove <u>lactic acid</u> from them (produced during <u>anaerobic</u> activity).
- To breathe out the extra <u>carbon dioxide</u> produced during aerobic activity.

Vital Capacity — the Most Air you can Breathe In

1) Your tidal volume is only a <u>fraction</u> of your <u>vital capacity</u>:

> <u>VITAL CAPACITY</u> — the most air you could possibly breathe in after breathing out the largest volume of air you can.

Don't panic if you see this definition with "in" and "out" swapped around — it makes no difference.

2) The <u>larger</u> your vital capacity, the <u>more oxygen</u> you can take in and absorb into your bloodstream in each breath — and the more oxygen you can <u>supply</u> to your muscles.

3) You can <u>increase</u> your vital capacity through exercise — see page 17.

4) Your vital capacity <u>isn't</u> the total volume of air in your lungs (your lung capacity). After you've <u>breathed out</u> as much as you can, there's still some air <u>left</u> in the lungs. This is called the <u>residual volume</u>.

Breathe iiiiiiiiiiiiiiiiin — and ooooooooouuuuuuut...

It's easy to get tidal volume and vital capacity mixed up — so make sure you keep revising their definitions until you can remember them without looking at this page. Here's an Exam Practice Question to have a go at.

Q1 Explain why an athlete would benefit from a high vital capacity. [3 marks]

Spirometers

A snazzy machine called a <u>spirometer</u> can tell you all sorts about the <u>lungs</u>, and what they're doing during <u>exercise</u>. You only need this page if you're doing the <u>AQA course</u> — if you're not, skip to the next page.

A Spirometer Trace shows Lung Air Volumes

You can measure the <u>volume</u> of air moving in and out of someone's lungs by getting them to breathe into a machine called a <u>spirometer</u>. A spirometer produces a <u>graph</u> called a <u>spirometer trace</u>.

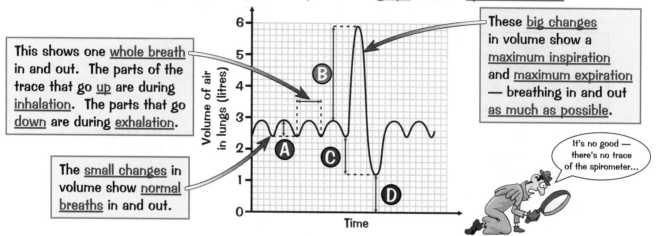

This shows one <u>whole breath</u> in and out. The parts of the trace that go <u>up</u> are during <u>inhalation</u>. The parts that go <u>down</u> are during <u>exhalation</u>.

These <u>big changes</u> in volume show a <u>maximum inspiration</u> and <u>maximum expiration</u> — breathing in and out <u>as much as possible</u>.

The <u>small changes</u> in volume show <u>normal breaths</u> in and out.

It's no good — there's no trace of the spirometer...

You need to be able to read some <u>lung volumes</u> from a spirometer trace:

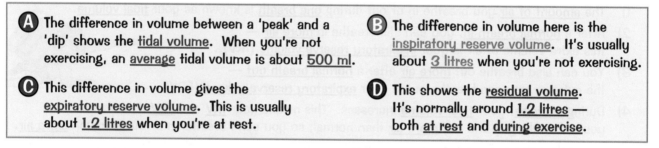

A The difference in volume between a 'peak' and a 'dip' shows the <u>tidal volume</u>. When you're not exercising, an <u>average</u> tidal volume is about <u>500 ml</u>.

B The difference in volume here is the <u>inspiratory reserve volume</u>. It's usually about <u>3 litres</u> when you're not exercising.

C This difference in volume gives the <u>expiratory reserve volume</u>. This is usually about <u>1.2 litres</u> when you're at rest.

D This shows the <u>residual volume</u>. It's normally around <u>1.2 litres</u> — both <u>at rest</u> and <u>during exercise</u>.

You can Analyse a Spirometer Trace

A spirometer trace can show you whether the person breathing into it was <u>resting</u> or <u>exercising</u>.

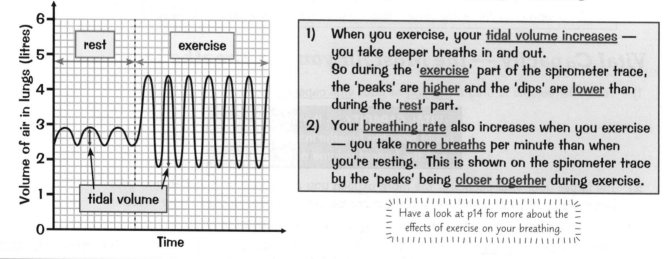

1) When you exercise, your <u>tidal volume increases</u> — you take deeper breaths in and out. So during the 'exercise' part of the spirometer trace, the 'peaks' are <u>higher</u> and the 'dips' are <u>lower</u> than during the '<u>rest</u>' part.

2) Your <u>breathing rate</u> also increases when you exercise — you take <u>more breaths</u> per minute than when you're resting. This is shown on the spirometer trace by the 'peaks' being <u>closer together</u> during exercise.

Have a look at p14 for more about the effects of exercise on your breathing.

I measured my lung volumes — they sounded pretty quiet to me...

You might need to draw a spirometer trace on a set of axes in your exam. But don't panic — just remember that the 'peaks' of the trace get taller and closer together during exercise, and you'll be fine. Try this Practice Question.

Q1 Look at the lung volume 'A' on the spirometer trace at the top of this page. Describe any changes to this volume during exercise and how they would appear on a spirometer trace.   [2 marks]

Aerobic and Anaerobic Exercise

Your body can release energy in different ways — it all depends on how hard and how long you're exercising. And different sources of fuel can be used to release energy in the muscles. Fantastic stuff.

Aerobic Activity — With Oxygen

1) All the living cells in your body need energy. Normally the body uses oxygen to release energy from glucose (a sugar found in food). This is called aerobic respiration.

Glucose + Oxygen → Carbon dioxide + Water + Energy

Carbon dioxide and water are by-products of aerobic respiration.

2) If your body's keeping up with the oxygen demand of its cells, it means there's enough oxygen available for aerobic respiration.

3) Activities where your body can keep up with oxygen demand are called aerobic activities.

4) You breathe out the carbon dioxide through your lungs, while the water is lost as sweat, urine, or in the air you breathe out.

AEROBIC ACTIVITY: 'with oxygen'. If the exercise you're doing isn't too fast and you're exercising at a steady rate, your heart and lungs can supply your muscles with all the oxygen they need.

5) As long as your muscles are supplied with enough oxygen, you can do aerobic exercise — so if you're exercising for long periods, you'll be producing your energy aerobically.

6) Aerobic respiration is how marathon runners get their energy — it's the most efficient way to get it.

Anaerobic Activity — Without Oxygen

1) During vigorous exercise, your body can't supply all the oxygen needed. When this happens, your muscles release energy without using oxygen in a different process called anaerobic respiration.

Glucose → Lactic acid + Energy

Lactic acid is a by-product of anaerobic respiration.

2) Activities where your body has to do this are called anaerobic activities.

ANAEROBIC ACTIVITY: 'without oxygen'. If you exercise in short, intense bursts, your heart and lungs can't supply your muscles with oxygen as fast as your cells use it.

3) The lack of oxygen during anaerobic respiration means it can only provide energy for short periods of time — so you can't exercise at high intensity for very long.

4) During the first few seconds of exercise (at any intensity), your muscles get energy anaerobically in a different way — using the 'ATP-PC' system. This just means they use an energy source called creatine phosphate, which is already stored in the muscles.

You only need to know about the ATP-PC system for the Eduqas course.

5) Creatine phosphate runs out very quickly. Once it's gone, your muscles will need to use aerobic or anaerobic respiration to release energy.

6) Sprinters get their energy anaerobically — they have to run quickly for short durations.

Carbohydrates and Fats are used as Fuel

1) Your body needs a source of fuel so that respiration can provide energy.

2) Carbohydrates (from foods such as pasta) and fats stored in the body can both be used as fuel.

CARBOHYDRATES — the body's main source of fuel. They're used during aerobic activities at moderate intensity and for high intensity anaerobic activities.

FATS — used as fuel for aerobic activity at low intensity. Fats provide more energy than carbohydrates, but they can't be used as fuel for higher intensity activities.

Have you met Anna Robic? She's an excellent sprinter...

You can adapt your training intensity based on whether you want to make your body better at exercising aerobically or anaerobically — have a look at page 34 to see how. Have a go at this Practice Question, too.

Q1 Justify why a 100 metre sprint would be an anaerobic activity. [3 marks]

Short-Term Effects of Exercise

Exercise has loads of different <u>short-term effects</u> on the body — some that <u>help</u> you to exercise, and others that are just a bit nasty. This page'll look at the effects on your <u>muscles</u> and your <u>breathing</u>.

There are Short-Term Effects on the Muscular System

There are loads of different effects on your muscles <u>during exercise</u>, and <u>straight after</u> it.

1) When you exercise, your muscles release <u>extra energy</u> for movement. Producing this energy also <u>generates heat</u>, which can make you feel <u>hot</u> and <u>sweaty</u>.

2) Also, during <u>anaerobic</u> activity, your muscles produce <u>lactic acid</u>. If you use your muscles <u>anaerobically</u> for too long, the lactic acid starts to <u>build up</u>. This leads to a rise in the <u>lactate levels</u> in the body — <u>lactate accumulation</u>.

3) Lactic acid build-up makes your muscles <u>painful</u> and causes <u>muscle fatigue</u> (tiredness).

4) If your muscles are <u>fatigued</u>, they need <u>oxygen</u> to <u>remove the lactic acid</u> and <u>recover</u>. The amount of <u>oxygen</u> you need is the <u>oxygen debt</u>, or '<u>EPOC</u>' — excess post-exercise oxygen consumption.

5) To <u>repay oxygen debt</u>, you'll need to <u>slow down</u> or <u>stop</u> the activity you're doing for a while, which can have a <u>negative</u> impact on your <u>performance</u>.

6) During a training session where you do <u>anaerobic activity</u>, you'll need to have periods of <u>rest</u> or <u>low intensity</u> exercise before you can work anaerobically again.

Working your muscles <u>really hard</u> during a workout can also affect your body <u>a day or two</u> after exercise.

1) You might feel <u>tired</u> because your muscles used up lots of <u>energy</u> during your workout.

2) You could also feel <u>sick</u> and <u>light-headed</u>.

3) Some people also get '<u>delayed onset of muscle soreness</u>' (DOMS), or <u>muscle cramp</u>.

There are Short-Term Effects on the Respiratory System

1) During exercise, <u>muscles</u> such as the <u>pectorals</u> and the <u>sternocleidomastoid</u> (in the neck) <u>expand</u> your lungs more to let in <u>extra air</u>. Muscles in your <u>abdomen</u> also work to pull your <u>ribcage</u> down and shrink the chest cavity quicker, so you <u>breathe out</u> faster.

2) These changes help to increase your <u>depth</u> of <u>breathing</u> and <u>rate</u> of <u>breathing</u> (the <u>number of breaths</u> per minute), which leads to an increase in your <u>minute ventilation</u> (or 'minute volume') — the <u>volume</u> of air you breathe in or out <u>each minute</u>.

Increasing your depth of breathing increases your <u>tidal volume</u> (see p11).

3) This means <u>more oxygen</u> is taken in and transferred to the blood, which helps to meet the <u>increased demand</u> for oxygen in the <u>muscles</u> during physical activity.

4) It also helps you to <u>breathe out</u> the extra <u>carbon dioxide</u> produced during aerobic respiration.

5) These changes allow you to do <u>aerobic activity</u> for <u>long periods</u> of time.

6) If you've been doing <u>anaerobic activity</u>, your breathing rate and depth will remain higher than normal until you've taken in enough <u>oxygen</u> to 'pay off' your <u>oxygen debt</u>.

These changes to your respiratory system will all be <u>more extreme</u> if you exercise really <u>intensely</u>. So you'll breathe <u>deeper</u> and <u>quicker</u> when you're exercising <u>hard</u> than when you're doing <u>light exercise</u>.

My brainular system feels fatigued...

It's not enough just knowing that you breathe faster and deeper during exercise — you need to know why, too. So remember, you need to get extra oxygen in, and extra carbon dioxide out. Now try an Exam Practice Question.

Q1 Outline how muscle fatigue may affect a player participating in a game of football. [1 mark]

Short-Term Effects of Exercise

Your cardiovascular system works extra hard during exercise to make sure your muscles get what they need to work properly. This includes using your blood vessels to send your blood where it's needed the most.

There are Short-Term Effects on the Cardiovascular System

1) Your heart rate is the number of times your heart beats per minute. An adult's resting heart rate (their heart rate when they aren't exercising) is usually about 60-80 bpm (beats per minute).

2) Your stroke volume is the amount of blood each ventricle pumps with each contraction (or heartbeat).

3) During exercise, your heart rate and stroke volume both increase.

4) This leads to an increase in your cardiac output — the volume of blood pumped by a ventricle per minute.

> cardiac output (Q) = heart rate × stroke volume

5) It also increases the pressure of your blood as your heart beats — your systolic blood pressure.

> Diastolic blood pressure is your blood's pressure when your heart is relaxed. It doesn't change much during exercise.

6) An increase in cardiac output increases the blood and oxygen supply to your muscles — so they can release the energy they need for physical activity. It also removes more carbon dioxide from the muscles and takes it to the lungs to be breathed out.

7) Your heart rate, stroke volume and cardiac output will remain higher than normal after exercise until any oxygen debt is paid off.

> The harder you're exercising, the higher your heart rate, stroke volume and cardiac output will be. So if you're only doing very light exercise, they'll be lower than if you were doing really strenuous exercise.

Your Blood Vessels Change when you Exercise

When you exercise, blood is redistributed around the body to increase the supply of oxygen to your muscles — this is known as 'vascular shunting'.

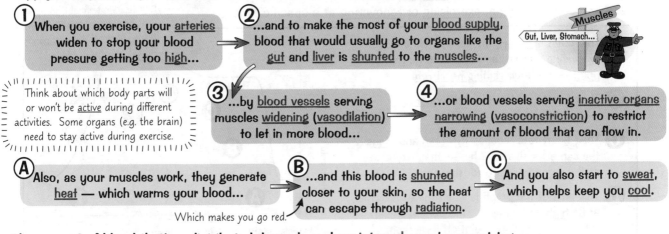

① When you exercise, your arteries widen to stop your blood pressure getting too high...

② ...and to make the most of your blood supply, blood that would usually go to organs like the gut and liver is shunted to the muscles...

Muscles
Gut, Liver, Stomach...

> Think about which body parts will or won't be active during different activities. Some organs (e.g. the brain) need to stay active during exercise.

③ ...by blood vessels serving muscles widening (vasodilation) to let in more blood...

④ ...or blood vessels serving inactive organs narrowing (vasoconstriction) to restrict the amount of blood that can flow in.

Ⓐ Also, as your muscles work, they generate heat — which warms your blood...

Ⓑ ...and this blood is shunted closer to your skin, so the heat can escape through radiation.

Which makes you go red.

Ⓒ And you also start to sweat, which helps keep you cool.

The amount of blood that's redistributed depends on how intensely you're exercising. So during light exercise, only a small amount of blood is shunted towards your working muscles. But if you're exercising really hard, a lot more blood is shunted.

Romantic comedies — exercise for your heart...

Remember, vascular shunting happens during exercise because your muscles need blood more than some of your organs do. And this couldn't happen without vasodilation and vasoconstriction. Now on to a Practice Question...

Q1 Copy and complete the following statements about the short-term effects of exercise.
During exercise, the .... and stroke volume increase. This leads to an increase in the .... output so more oxygenated .... is delivered to the muscles. [3 marks]

Q2 Explain why vasoconstriction occurs in the blood vessels of the stomach during physical activity and sport. [3 marks]

Short-Term Effects of Exercise

This page'll show you how the <u>cardiovascular</u> and <u>respiratory</u> systems <u>team up</u> to help you exercise.
It'll also give you some handy tips on how to <u>interpret exercise data</u> that you might see in the exam.

The Cardiovascular and Respiratory Systems Work Together

1) During exercise (and immediately after), <u>more oxygen</u> is delivered to the muscles than normal. Extra <u>carbon dioxide</u> is also taken away from them and <u>breathed out</u>.

2) The <u>cardiovascular</u> and <u>respiratory</u> systems work together to make this happen. When you exercise:

MORE O$_2$ DELIVERED

1) <u>Breathing rate</u> and <u>depth</u> increase, so more oxygen is delivered to the <u>alveoli</u> in the lungs.

2) <u>Cardiac output</u> also increases — so <u>blood</u> passes through the lungs at a <u>faster rate</u>, and picks up the <u>extra oxygen</u> from the <u>alveoli</u>. It's then delivered to the <u>muscles</u>.

MORE CO$_2$ REMOVED

1) Increased <u>cardiac output</u> means that the blood can transport <u>carbon dioxide</u> from the <u>muscles</u> to the <u>lungs</u> more <u>quickly</u>.

2) Here it moves back into the <u>alveoli</u>, and the higher <u>breathing rate</u> and <u>depth</u> allow it to be quickly <u>breathed out</u>.

3) These changes create a <u>high concentration gradient</u> — after you breathe in, there's a lot <u>more oxygen</u> in the <u>alveoli</u> than the capillaries, and a lot <u>more carbon dioxide</u> in the <u>capillaries</u> than the alveoli.

4) This causes <u>diffusion</u> of the gases to happen <u>much quicker</u> during exercise.

5) These processes help you to release enough <u>energy</u> to <u>exercise</u> aerobically and to <u>recover</u> from <u>oxygen debt</u> after anaerobic activity (see p14).

For more on diffusion, have a look at page 10.

Short-Term Effects can be shown Graphically

1) In your exam, you might get a graph or table showing someone's <u>heart rate</u>, <u>stroke volume</u> or <u>cardiac output</u> during a workout.

2) These things all <u>increase</u> when you exercise, and gradually go <u>back to normal</u> once you stop exercising.

3) You can use these facts to <u>interpret</u> data and work out whether a person was <u>resting</u>, <u>exercising</u> or <u>recovering</u> at a specific time.

Your <u>heart rate</u> might go up slightly just <u>before</u> you start exercising — this is known as an <u>anticipatory rise</u>.

A) This point is <u>before</u> the person has started exercising. Their heart rate is at its <u>lowest point</u> — it's their <u>resting heart rate</u>.

B) Their heart rate has started to <u>increase</u> — they've started to exercise.

C) Their heart rate reaches <u>130 bpm</u> and <u>stays the same</u> for five minutes — they exercise at the <u>same intensity</u> for that time.

D) This part of the graph is when the workout is at its <u>highest intensity</u>. The person's heart rate is at its <u>highest</u> point on the graph.

E) Their heart rate is <u>decreasing</u> — exercise has <u>stopped</u>, or they're completing a <u>cool down</u>. Their heart rate <u>stays fairly high</u> for a while to help with <u>recovery</u>.

F) They've returned to their <u>resting</u> heart rate of 70 beats per minute.

Graphs and tables? I didn't sign up for extra maths lessons...

I bet you weren't pleased to see a graph on this page, but it's not too bad. If you get given any heart rate, stroke volume or cardiac output data in your exam, remember that they all go up during exercise, and back down afterwards. Then you can work out what was going on when the values were recorded. Try this Practice Question.

Q1 The table on the right shows an athlete's stroke volume recorded three times during a training session. Identify which value was recorded:

| 94 cm³ | 141 cm³ | 63 cm³ |

a) before exercise started   [1 mark]   b) during high-intensity exercise   [1 mark]

Long-Term Effects of Exercise

Exercising regularly eventually leads to loads of adaptations in the body's systems. These benefit your health and different components of fitness (see pages 23-26), which will help improve your performance.

Exercise Improves the Musculo-Skeletal System

MUSCLE HYPERTROPHY

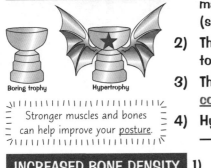

Boring trophy   Hypertrophy

Stronger muscles and bones can help improve your posture.

1) Doing regular exercise (especially resistance training) will make your muscles thicker and your muscle girth larger (see p53) — which can change your body shape.

2) This thickening of muscles is called hypertrophy. It happens to all muscles when they're exercised, including your heart.

3) The thicker a muscle is, the more strongly it can contract — so this increases your strength.

4) Hypertrophy also improves your muscular endurance — so you can use your muscles for longer.

See p45-46 for more about the long-term benefits of exercise.

Anaerobic training improves your muscles' ability to work without oxygen.

INCREASED BONE DENSITY

1) The denser your bones, the stronger they are.

2) Exercise usually puts stress or forces through bones, and will cause the body to strengthen those bones.

3) The stronger your bones, the less likely they are to break or fracture.

STRONGER LIGAMENTS & TENDONS Having stronger ligaments and tendons can make you more flexible and less likely to injure yourself, e.g. dislocation (see p41).

Exercise Improves the Cardio-Respiratory System

BIGGER/STRONGER HEART

1) Your heart is just a muscle — when you exercise, it adapts and gets bigger and stronger.

2) A bigger, stronger heart will contract more strongly and pump more blood with each beat — so your resting stroke volume and maximum cardiac output will increase.

3) A larger stroke volume means your heart has to beat less often to pump the same amount of blood around your body. This means your resting heart rate decreases.

This is called 'cardiac hypertrophy'.

This is called 'bradycardia'.

LARGER LUNG CAPACITY

1) Your diaphragm and external intercostal muscles (the muscles between the ribs) get stronger — so they can make your chest cavity larger. The number of alveoli in your lungs also increases.

2) This increases your maximum tidal volume and minute ventilation during exercise. Your vital capacity and lung capacity increase — you can breathe in more air.

3) The larger your lung capacity, the more oxygen you can get into your lungs and into your bloodstream per breath — so you can take in the same amount of oxygen with a lower breathing rate.

LOWER BLOOD PRESSURE

With regular exercise, your veins and arteries get bigger and their muscular walls become more elastic — so your blood pressure falls.

MORE CAPILLARIES IN THE MUSCLES

This increases the blood supply to the muscles, so they receive more oxygen.

MORE RED BLOOD CELLS

So the blood can carry more oxygen.

The better the blood and oxygen supply to your muscles, the better your cardiovascular fitness is. This means you can exercise more intensely and for longer, as well as recover more quickly after exercise.

Training that involves aerobic activity works best to improve the cardio-respiratory system.

Breaking news — exercise is good for you...

To get all these lovely long-term effects, you'll need to rest after exercise so that you can recover and let your body adapt to any changes. Here's the last Exam Practice Question in this section for you to try. Have fun...

Q1 Justify why muscle hypertrophy would benefit a performer participating in weightlifting.   [3 marks]

Revision Questions For Section One

Well, that's <u>Anatomy and Physiology</u> all wrapped up — time to see <u>how much you know</u> about the body.
- Try these questions and <u>tick off each one</u> when you <u>get it right</u>.
- When you've done <u>all the questions</u> for a topic and are <u>completely happy</u> with it, tick off the topic.
- The answers can all be found by <u>looking back over pages 1 to 17</u>.

The Musculo-Skeletal System (p1-7) ☑

1) Name the five main functions of the skeleton. ☑
2) State the four main types of bone in the body. ☑
3) Name the five regions of the vertebral column. ☑
4) Which two bones meet to make the hip joint? ☑
5) Which joint movement involves pointing the toes upwards? ☑
6) Give an example of a condyloid joint. ☑
7) What is the function of:
    a) Cartilage?
    b) Ligaments?
    c) Tendons? ☑
8) What is the function of the synovial membrane within a joint? ☑
9) Which type of muscle is involved in moving the skeleton — voluntary, involuntary, or cardiac? ☑
10) Which two muscles make up the antagonistic muscle pair operating at the elbow joint? ☑
11) What is the difference between an isometric and an isotonic muscle contraction? ☑
12) Why would type IIA and IIX muscle fibres not be suitable for use in a marathon? ☑

The Cardio-Respiratory System (p8-12) ☐

13) What are the three main functions of the cardiovascular system? ☑
14) Which vein does deoxygenated blood pass through to enter the heart? ☑
15) The pulmonary artery carries oxygenated blood to the rest of the body. TRUE or FALSE? ☑
16) Name the three main types of blood vessel found in the body. ☑
17) What is the function of plasma? ☑
18) Explain how oxygen and carbon dioxide are exchanged between the alveoli and capillaries. ☑
19) Give the compositions of inhaled and exhaled air. ☑
20) Describe what is meant by a) tidal volume, and b) vital capacity. ☑

Aerobic and Anaerobic Exercise (p13) ☑

21) Describe aerobic and anaerobic respiration. ☑
22) What is the main fuel source used in both aerobic and anaerobic activity? ☑

The Short-Term and Long-Term Effects of Exercise (p14-17) ☑

23) Why do muscles become fatigued during anaerobic activity, and how do they recover? ☑
24) Explain why your depth and rate of breathing increase during exercise. ☑
25) Why do heart rate, stroke volume and cardiac output remain higher after exercise? ☑
26) Explain what vasodilation and vasoconstriction are and why they happen. ☑
27) What is muscle hypertrophy and why does it happen? ☑
28) How does regular exercise benefit the bones, ligaments and tendons? ☑
29) Explain why regular exercise leads to increased oxygen supply to the muscles. ☑

Lever Systems

When the <u>muscular</u> and <u>skeletal systems</u> work together, they create <u>lever systems</u> that help us to <u>move</u>.

Lever Systems Help the Body to Move

A <u>lever</u> is a <u>solid bar</u> that moves about a <u>fixed point</u> when <u>force</u> is applied to it.
When a <u>muscle</u> pulls on a <u>bone</u> to move a body part about a <u>joint</u>, it uses the body part as a <u>lever</u>.
This lever makes up part of a <u>lever system</u> that has <u>four</u> different components:

1) The <u>lever arm</u> — the <u>bone</u> or <u>body part</u> being moved about a point.
   On a diagram of a lever system, it's shown as a <u>straight line</u>.

2) The <u>fulcrum</u> — the <u>joint</u> where the lever arm <u>pivots</u>. It's shown as a <u>triangle</u>.

3) The <u>effort</u> — the <u>force</u> applied by the <u>muscles</u> to the lever arm. It's shown
   by an <u>arrow</u> pointing in the direction of the force. The <u>perpendicular distance</u>
   between the fulcrum and the action of the effort is the '<u>effort arm</u>'.

   > 'Perpendicular' means
   > 'at 90 degrees to'.

4) The <u>load</u> — the <u>resistance</u> against the pull of the muscles on the lever arm. E.g. the weight of the body,
   or body part, or something being lifted. A <u>square</u> or an <u>arrow</u> is used to represent the load. The <u>perpendicular</u>
   <u>distance</u> between the fulcrum and the action of the load is the '<u>weight arm</u>' (or 'resistance arm').

There are <u>three</u> types of lever system:

| **1ST CLASS** — The <u>load</u> and <u>effort</u> are at <u>opposite ends</u> of the lever. The fulcrum is in the middle. | **2ND CLASS** — The <u>fulcrum</u> and <u>effort</u> are at <u>opposite ends</u> of the lever. The load is in the middle. | **3RD CLASS** — The <u>fulcrum</u> and <u>load</u> are at <u>opposite ends</u> of the lever. The effort is in the middle. |

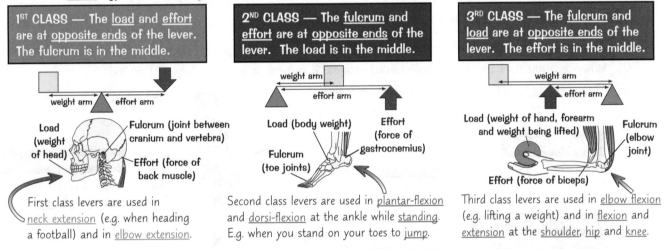

First class levers are used in <u>neck extension</u> (e.g. when heading a football) and in <u>elbow extension</u>.

Second class levers are used in <u>plantar-flexion</u> and <u>dorsi-flexion</u> at the ankle while <u>standing</u>. E.g. when you stand on your toes to <u>jump</u>.

Third class levers are used in <u>elbow flexion</u> (e.g. lifting a weight) and in <u>flexion</u> and <u>extension</u> at the <u>shoulder</u>, <u>hip</u> and <u>knee</u>.

Levers can have a Mechanical Advantage or Disadvantage

Levers <u>help</u> the body use its muscles <u>effectively</u>. Different levers have <u>different benefits</u> — some help to move <u>heavier loads</u>, while others increase the <u>speed</u> a load can be moved at, or the <u>range of movement</u>.

1) A lever in the body with a <u>mechanical advantage</u> can move a <u>large load</u> with a <u>small effort</u> from the muscles. However, it can only move the load <u>short distances</u> at <u>low speeds</u>.

   > If the <u>effort arm</u> is <u>longer</u> than the <u>weight arm</u>, the lever has a <u>mechanical advantage</u> (MA).

2) <u>Second class</u> levers always have a <u>mechanical advantage</u> — the <u>effort</u> arm is always longer than the <u>weight</u> arm.

   > MA = effort arm ÷ weight arm

3) A <u>first class lever</u> has a <u>mechanical advantage</u> if the <u>fulcrum</u> is closer to the <u>load</u> than it is to the <u>effort</u>.

4) A lever with a <u>mechanical disadvantage</u> requires a <u>large effort</u> from the muscles to move a <u>small load</u> — but it can move the load <u>quickly</u> through a <u>large range of movement</u>.

5) <u>Third class levers</u> always have a <u>mechanical disadvantage</u> — the <u>effort arm</u> is always shorter than the <u>weight arm</u>.

6) A <u>first class lever</u> has a <u>mechanical disadvantage</u> if the <u>fulcrum</u> is closer to the <u>effort</u> than it is to the <u>load</u>.

Moving joints — you'd better lever little space...

To remember the lever classes, use '1, 2, 3, F, L, E'. The letters tell you the middle component of each lever — for 1st class it's the <u>fulcrum</u>, for 2nd class it's the <u>load</u>, and for 3rd class it's the <u>effort</u>. Try this Practice Question.

Q1   State the lever class operating at the elbow when the ball is released during a football throw-in.   [1 mark]

Planes and Axes of Movement

It might seem a bit odd that there's a page about planes and axes in a PE book — but it'll all make sense soon. Basically, you can describe a body movement using the <u>plane</u> it <u>moves in</u> and the <u>axis</u> it <u>moves around</u>.

Movements Happen In Planes

1) A plane of movement is an imaginary <u>flat surface</u> which runs through the body.

2) Planes are used to describe the <u>direction</u> of a movement.

3) When you move a body part (or your whole body), it moves <u>in a plane</u>.

4) There are <u>three</u> planes of movement you need to know:

SAGITTAL PLANE
Divides the body into <u>left</u> and <u>right</u> sides.

TRANSVERSE PLANE
Divides the body into <u>top</u> and <u>bottom</u>.

FRONTAL PLANE
Divides the body's <u>front</u> and <u>back</u>.

Movements Happen Around Axes

1) An axis of movement (two or more are called '<u>axes</u>') is an <u>imaginary line</u> which runs through the body.

2) When a body part (or your whole body) moves, it moves <u>around</u> (or '<u>about</u>') an axis.

3) There are <u>three</u> types of axis you need to know:

For the <u>OCR</u> course, this is called the <u>frontal axis</u>.

For the <u>Edexcel</u> or <u>Eduqas</u> course, this is called the <u>frontal axis</u>.

SAGITTAL AXIS
Runs through the body from <u>front to back</u>.

TRANSVERSE AXIS
Runs through the body from <u>left to right</u>.

For the <u>Edexcel</u> or <u>Eduqas</u> course, this is called the <u>vertical axis</u>.

LONGITUDINAL AXIS
Runs through the body from <u>top to bottom</u>.

Movements use Different Planes and Axes

Every body movement uses <u>both</u> a <u>plane</u> and an <u>axis</u>.
Learn the plane and axis <u>pairs</u> for these <u>movement types</u> and <u>sporting examples</u>.

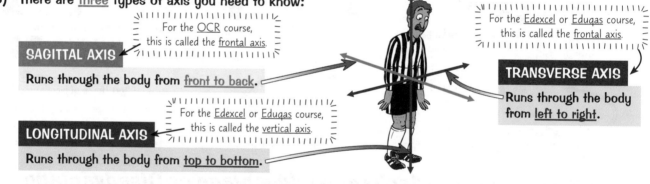

MOVEMENT TYPE	PLANE	AXIS	SPORT MOVEMENTS
flexion/extension	sagittal	transverse	tucked and piked somersaults, running, forward roll
abduction/adduction	frontal	sagittal	cartwheel
rotation	transverse	longitudinal	full twist jump (trampolining), discus throw rotation, ice skating spin

Have a look at page 3 for more examples of the movement types.

These plane and axis pairs are always <u>the same</u>, e.g. movements that happen in the <u>transverse plane</u> always happen around the <u>longitudinal/vertical axis</u>.

Movement in planes — only when the seatbelt signs are off...

Don't forget, the plane and axis combinations are always the same — so make sure you learn the pairs for your exam, and that you know the right axis names for your course, too. Have a go at this Exam Practice Question.

Q1   State the plane and axis used during a star jump.

[2 marks]

Revision Questions for Section Two

Well, Section Two was short and sweet... Try these revision questions to make sure you took it all in.
- Try these questions and tick off each one when you get it right.
- When you've done all the questions for a topic and are completely happy with it, tick off the topic.
- The answers can all be found by looking back over pages 19 and 20.

Lever Systems (p19) ☑

1) Name the four components of a lever system. ☑
2) What is the effort arm of a lever? What is the weight arm? ☑
3) State the class of each of the levers below.

   a) 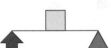   b)    c)

4) Give two examples of first class levers in the body. ☑
5) Which class of lever is used in the foot when jumping? ☑
6) Which lever class is used during elbow flexion? ☑
7) Explain what is meant if a lever system in the body has a:
   a) mechanical advantage
   b) mechanical disadvantage ☑
8) How do you calculate the mechanical advantage of a lever? ☑
9) Which class of lever always has a:
   a) mechanical advantage?
   b) mechanical disadvantage? ☑
10) When does a first class lever have a mechanical advantage? ☑

Planes and Axes of Movement (p20) ☐

11) What is a plane of movement? ☑
12) Which plane of movement divides:
   a) the top and bottom of the body?
   b) the left and right sides of the body?
   c) the front and back of the body? ☑
13) What is an axis of movement? ☑
14) Which axis runs through the body from:
   a) top to bottom?
   b) front to back?
   c) left to right? ☑
15) Which plane and axis are used during both tucked and piked somersaults? ☑
16) Which plane and axis are used during a cartwheel? ☑
17) Which plane and axis are used during a full twist jump in trampolining? ☑

Health and Fitness

We'll start with <u>telekinesis</u>, then a bit of <u>mind-reading</u>... Sorry, I thought this section was <u>Psychical Training</u>.
Try again... First up, four important words: <u>health</u>, <u>fitness</u>, <u>exercise</u> and how they affect <u>performance</u>.

Fitness is just One Part of being Healthy

1)   Being healthy is <u>more</u> than just having a healthy body. Don't take my word for it though —
here's the definition used by the <u>World Health Organisation</u> (WHO):

> <u>Health</u> is a state of complete <u>physical</u>, <u>mental</u> and <u>social well-being</u>
> and <u>not</u> merely the absence of disease or infirmity.

2)   <u>Fitness</u> is one part of <u>good health</u> — here's the definition:

> <u>Fitness</u> is the ability to meet the <u>demands of the environment</u>.

So, being fit means you're <u>physically able</u> to do whatever you <u>want</u> or <u>need</u> to do,
without getting tired quickly.

3)   Fitness <u>helps</u> with <u>physical</u> health, but you can have a <u>high</u> level of fitness <u>without</u> necessarily being
physically healthy — e.g. some athletes <u>overtrain</u> and end up getting <u>injured</u>.

4)   <u>Mental</u> and <u>social</u> well-being is also part of being healthy —
if you're always unhappy, then you're not healthy.

Exercise Keeps You Fit and Healthy

> <u>Exercise</u> is a form of physical activity done to <u>maintain</u> or <u>improve health</u> and/or <u>fitness</u>.

It <u>doesn't</u> have to be a <u>competitive sport</u>.

1)   By exercising, you can improve <u>components of fitness</u> (see p23-26) and general <u>physical health</u>.

2)   As well as keeping you physically fit, exercise also helps with <u>emotional</u> and <u>social</u> well-being:

   •   Exercise is a good <u>stress relief</u> and is <u>enjoyable</u>.

   •   Exercise can be a <u>social activity</u> — e.g. joining a yoga class
   can help you make <u>new friends</u> or socialise with <u>current friends</u>.

See p46 for more about how exercise helps emotional and social well-being.

You need to be Fit and Healthy to Perform Well

1)   Your level of health and fitness will <u>affect</u> your <u>performance</u>.

> <u>Performance</u> is <u>how well</u> a task is completed.

2)   Your performance won't be as good if you're <u>unfit</u> — e.g. in the
<u>second half</u> of a football match you'll get tired and be less <u>effective</u>.

3)   Being <u>unhealthy</u> will also affect performance — if you have the <u>flu</u>, playing sport is going to be <u>tricky</u>...

Gary's performance left many wondering about his emotional well-being.

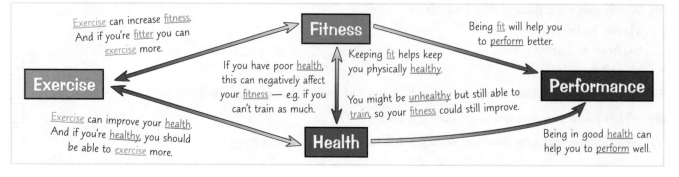

<u>Exercise</u> can increase <u>fitness</u>.
And if you're <u>fitter</u> you can
<u>exercise</u> more.

Being <u>fit</u> will help you
to <u>perform</u> better.

Fitness

If you have poor <u>health</u>,
this can negatively affect
your <u>fitness</u> — e.g. if you
can't train as much.

Keeping <u>fit</u> helps keep
you physically <u>healthy</u>.

You might be <u>unhealthy</u> but still able to
<u>train</u>, so your <u>fitness</u> could still improve.

Exercise

Performance

<u>Exercise</u> can improve your <u>health</u>.
And if you're <u>healthy</u>, you should
be able to <u>exercise</u> more.

Health

Being in good <u>health</u> can
help you to <u>perform</u> well.

Health is wealth — you can't buy biscuits with well-being though...

You can see from that rather wonderful diagram (if I say so myself) that these things are all related, and exercise is
the key to improving health, fitness and performance. Now, have a go at this Exam Practice Question...

Q1   Explain how an athlete could have a high level of fitness, but still be unhealthy.   [2 marks]

Components of Fitness

Fitness can be split up into different components. Six of these components are needed to cope with the physical demands of an activity or sport. Here are the first three, so hop to it and get learning...

Cardiovascular Endurance — Getting Oxygen to the Muscles

1) Your heart and lungs work together to keep your muscles supplied with oxygen. The harder you work your muscles, the more oxygen they need.

> **CARDIOVASCULAR ENDURANCE** is the ability of the heart and lungs to supply oxygen to the muscles, so that the whole body can be exercised for a long time.

There are lots of different terms that mean the same thing. You might also see cardiovascular fitness, aerobic endurance, aerobic power or stamina.

2) So if you have a high level of cardiovascular endurance, your body is able to supply the oxygen your muscles need to do moderately intense whole-body exercise for a long time.

3) Most sports require good cardiovascular endurance. For example, a squash player needs to be able to keep up a fast pace all game. If a tennis player finds they are getting tired and losing points late on in a match, they will want to work on their cardiovascular endurance.

4) A high level of cardiovascular endurance is particularly important for endurance sports like long-distance running, or cycling.

Strength — the Force a Muscle can Exert

1) Strength is just how strong your muscles are.

> **STRENGTH** is the amount of force that a muscle or muscle group can apply against a resistance.

You might see 'muscular strength' instead of 'strength' — don't panic though, it's the same thing.

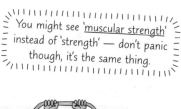

2) It's very important in sports where you need to lift, push or pull things using a lot of force, like weightlifting and judo.

3) Sports that require you to hold your own body weight also need a lot of strength — like the parallel bars and rings in gymnastics.

4) Strength can be broken down into different types:

- Maximal strength is the most amount of force a muscle group can create in a single movement.
- Static strength is when the muscles don't move, but still apply a force — e.g. when holding a handstand.
- Explosive strength uses a muscle's strength in a short, fast burst — it's similar to power (see p26).
- Dynamic strength means using your strength to move things repeatedly. It's like muscular endurance...

Muscular Endurance — How Long 'til You get Tired

1) When you work your muscles they can get tired and start to feel heavy and weak (fatigued).

> **MUSCULAR ENDURANCE** is the ability to repeatedly use muscles over a long time, without getting tired.

2) Muscular endurance is really important in any physical activity where you're using the same muscles over and over again — e.g. in racquet sports like tennis or squash where you have to repeatedly swing your arm.

3) It's also dead important towards the end of any long-distance race — rowers and cyclists need muscular endurance for a strong sprint finish.

Dave's muscular endurance was low — his arm felt heavy after 3 swigs of tea.

'Be strong Luke — apply the force against a resistance...'

Make sure you're specific about how components of fitness are used in different activities — e.g. instead of just saying 'strength helps in gymnastics' say 'strength helps the gymnast hold their body weight on the parallel bars'.

Q1 Assess the importance of muscular endurance for a long-distance cyclist.　　　　[3 marks]

Components of Fitness

Three more components of fitness on this page: <u>flexibility</u>, <u>body composition</u> and <u>speed</u>. Learn what they are — then make sure you learn what sports and activities each one's important in as well. Right, here we go...

Flexibility — Range of Movement

1) Flexibility is to do with <u>how far</u> your joints move. This depends on the <u>type of joint</u> and the 'stretchiness' of the <u>muscles</u> around it.

> **FLEXIBILITY** is the <u>amount of movement</u> possible at a <u>joint</u>.

He'll bend over backwards to help you, you know.

So I've heard.

2) It's often forgotten about, but <u>flexibility</u> is dead useful for <u>any</u> physical activity. Here's why...

- **FEWER INJURIES:**
  If you're <u>flexible</u>, you're <u>less likely</u> to <u>pull</u> or <u>strain</u> a muscle or stretch too far and injure yourself.

- **BETTER PERFORMANCE:**
  You can't do some activities <u>without</u> being flexible — e.g. doing the <u>splits</u> in <u>gymnastics</u>.

  Flexibility makes you <u>more efficient</u> in other sports so you use less <u>energy</u> — e.g. <u>swimmers</u> with better flexibility can move their arms <u>further</u> around their <u>shoulders</u>. This makes their strokes <u>longer</u> and <u>smoother</u>.

- **BETTER POSTURE:**
  Bad posture can <u>impair breathing</u> and damage your <u>spine</u>.

  More flexibility means a <u>better posture</u> and <u>fewer aches and pains</u>.

It took me years to get this flexible.

Body Composition — % of Fat, Muscle and Bone

> <u>BODY COMPOSITION</u> is the <u>percentage</u> of body weight made up by <u>fat, muscle and bone</u>.

1) If you're healthy, your body will normally be made up of between <u>15%</u> and <u>25% body fat</u>.
2) Having too much body fat can put <u>strain</u> on your <u>muscles</u> and <u>joints</u> during physical activity.
3) Different activities and sports demand <u>different</u> body compositions, depending on whether you need to be heavy, light, strong, fast, etc.

   Many physical activities become <u>harder</u> to do, and the increased strain on your body means you have a <u>higher risk</u> of <u>injuring</u> yourself.

- <u>Rock climbers</u> have to be <u>light</u> and <u>strong</u>, so have a <u>high muscle</u> percentage, and a <u>low body fat</u> percentage.
- In <u>rugby</u> or <u>American football</u>, <u>heavy</u> players have an advantage as they are <u>harder to knock over</u>, so will have a higher <u>body fat</u> percentage than many other sports players.

Speed — How Quickly

1) <u>Speed</u> is a measure of how <u>quickly</u> you can do something.
2) This might be a measure of how quickly you <u>cover a distance</u>. It could also be how quickly you can <u>carry out a movement</u>, e.g. how quickly you can throw a punch.
3) To work out speed, you just <u>divide</u> the <u>distance</u> covered by the <u>time</u> taken to do it.
4) Speed is important in lots of activities, from the obvious like a <u>100 m sprint</u>, to the less obvious (like the speed a hockey player can <u>swing their arm</u> to whack a ball across the pitch).

> <u>SPEED</u> is the <u>rate</u> at which someone is able to <u>move</u>, or to cover a <u>distance</u> in a given amount of <u>time</u>.

I like to think my body composition is 20% fat, 80% hero...

List some sports and then write down the components of fitness that are useful for each sport. I know it's not as fun as playing the sports, but you'll be laughing come exam time. Now, practice makes perfect and all that...

Q1 Give **two** ways that better flexibility can help a swimmer's performance.   [2 marks]

Components of Fitness

Now it's time to look at five components of fitness that require skill. Just like the more physical ones, you need to be able to judge their importance for different activities. First up — agility, balance and coordination.

Agility — Control Over Your Body's Movement

1) Agility is important in any activity where you've got to run about, changing direction all the time, like football or hockey.

2) Jumping and intercepting a pass in netball or basketball involves a high level of agility too.

AGILITY is the ability to change body position or direction quickly and with control.

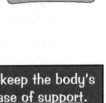

Balance — More Than Not Wobbling

Having a good sense of balance means you don't wobble or fall over easily. Here's a slightly fancier definition.

BALANCE is the ability to keep the body's centre of mass over a base of support.

1) You can think of the mass of any object as being concentrated at just one point. This point is called the centre of mass (or centre of gravity).

2) Everything has a centre of mass — and that includes us.

3) As you change body position, the location of your centre of mass will change too.

4) Whatever activity you're doing, you need to have your centre of mass over whatever is supporting you (your base of support) to balance. If you don't, you'll fall over.

This is true whether you're moving (dynamic balance)...

...changing orientation and shape (like in dance and gymnastics)...

...or just staying still (stationary or static balance).

Base of support: Geoff
centre of mass

Base of support: arms

Show-off...
Base of support: legs

5) Balance is crucial for nearly every physical activity. Any sport that involves changing direction quickly — like football or basketball — requires good balance.

6) An action that is performed with balance is more efficient — e.g. a cyclist might work on improving their balance to increase the speed they can go round corners.

Coordination — Using Body Parts Together

COORDINATION is the ability to use two or more parts of the body together, efficiently and accurately.

1) Hand-eye coordination is important in sports that require precision. E.g. being able to hit a ball in tennis, or shoot a bull's-eye in archery.

2) Limb coordination allows you to be able to walk, run, dance, kick, swim...

3) Coordinated movements are smooth and efficient. E.g. a runner with well coordinated arms and legs will be able to run faster than someone who is less coordinated.

4) Limb coordination is really important in sports like gymnastics or platform diving, where your performance is judged on your coordination.

Agility, Balance and Coordination — as easy as ABC...

Agility, balance and coordination all go together really. You can't be agile if you're not balanced and coordinated. Learn the definitions and how they apply to different activities, then try this Exam Practice Question.

Q1 Explain what is meant by coordination. Give an example of a boxer using coordination. [2 marks]

Components of Fitness

You're nearly there now, just two more components to go. Now you have the <u>agility</u>, <u>balance</u> and <u>coordination</u> of a ninja, what's next? How about cat-like <u>reactions</u> and ~~super~~<u>power</u>(s)? Sorry, I'm getting carried away...

Reaction Time — The Time It Takes You to React

<u>REACTION TIME</u> is the <u>time</u> taken to <u>move in response</u> to a <u>stimulus</u>.

1) In many sports and activities, you need to have <u>fast reactions</u>.
2) The <u>stimulus</u> you respond to could be, e.g., a <u>starter gun</u>, a <u>pass</u> in football, or a <u>serve</u> in tennis.
3) You need fast reactions to be able to <u>hit a ball</u> or <u>dodge a punch</u>. It doesn't matter how fast you can move, if you don't <u>react in time</u> you'll miss or get hit.
4) Having fast reactions can effectively give you a <u>head start</u>.

Getting away quickly at the start of a <u>sprint</u> can mean the difference between winning and losing.

Having <u>faster</u> reactions in team sports can help you <u>get away</u> from your opponents, so you can get into better playing <u>positions</u>.

Power Means Speed and Strength Together

<u>POWER</u> is a combination of <u>speed</u> and <u>strength</u>.

<u>power</u> = <u>strength</u> × <u>speed</u>

Most sports need power for some things. It's important for <u>throwing</u>, <u>hitting</u>, <u>sprinting</u> and <u>jumping</u> — e.g. in the <u>long jump</u>, both the sprint <u>run-up</u> and the <u>take-off</u> from the board require <u>power</u>. Here are some more examples:

I have the power.

SPORT	YOU NEED POWER TO...
Football	...shoot
Golf	...drive
Table tennis	...smash
Tennis	...serve and smash
Cricket	...bowl fast and bat

<u>Coordination</u> and <u>balance</u> also help make the most of power — an <u>uncoordinated</u> or <u>off-balance</u> action will <u>not</u> be as powerful.

Some Components are More Important than Others

1) To be good at <u>any</u> physical activity, you're going to need to have a <u>high level</u> of a <u>number</u> of different <u>components</u> of fitness.
2) For a particular activity, there will always be some components of fitness which are <u>more important</u> than others — e.g. in <u>weightlifting</u>, your <u>strength</u> is more important than your <u>reaction time</u>.
3) To compare the importance of different components, think about the <u>kinds of actions</u> the performer does — e.g. a batsman in <u>cricket</u> has to <u>react</u> to the bowler (<u>reaction time</u>), <u>hit</u> the ball (<u>coordination</u> and <u>power</u>), and then <u>run</u> (<u>speed</u> and <u>cardiovascular endurance</u>).

Revise more I tell you — sorry, all this power's gone to my head...

Congratulations, you've made it. No more components of fitness to learn. You know the drill — make sure you understand what each component is and which activities it's important in. Then it's Practice Question time.

Q1 Give **two** examples of a player using power in rugby. [2 marks]

Fitness Testing

So, you know what the components of fitness are — now you need to know how to measure them. Read on to find out why your PE teacher made you do the stupid bleep test at 9 am in the pouring rain*.

Fitness Testing Helps Identify Strengths and Weaknesses

Fitness testing gives you data that you can analyse to help improve your fitness.

1) Fitness tests are designed to measure specific components of fitness. It's important you choose the right one for the specific component you're interested in — otherwise the test is meaningless.

2) You can use fitness testing to measure your level of fitness before starting a training programme. The data will show your strengths and weaknesses, so you can plan a personal exercise programme (see p32) that focuses on what you need to improve. Some of the tests are quite demanding, so you need to make sure you are fit enough to manage them.

3) The data from fitness tests can be compared with national averages (see p31).

4) You can carry out fitness tests throughout a training programme to monitor your progress and see whether or not the training you're doing is working. This can help to motivate you by showing you where you're improving, and can help you to set yourself new goals.

Tests need to be carried out using the same procedure each time so comparisons with previous tests are meaningful.

These Three Tests are for Cardiovascular Endurance...

HARVARD STEP TEST

Equipment needed: stopwatch and 45 cm step.

1) Do 30 step-ups a minute (that's a step every two seconds) for 5 minutes.

2) Then take three pulse readings: the first one minute after you finish the test, the second two minutes after and the third three minutes after.

3) Put these numbers into a clever formula to work out your score — the higher your score, the better your cardiovascular endurance.

4) There are different versions of this test — check the procedures match before you compare results from different tests.

This new Harvard Step Test is just step-tastic

You might know this one as the 'bleep test'. Make sure to use its proper name in the exam though.

For the swim test, you'll need a pool instead of a 400 m track...

COOPER 12-MINUTE RUN AND SWIM TESTS

I've only got room to describe the run test here — the swim test's the same, just wetter...

Equipment needed: stopwatch and a 400 m track.

1) Run round a track as many times as you can in 12 minutes (or walk if you get too tired to run).

2) The distance you run/walk is recorded in metres. The further it is, the better your cardiovascular endurance.

MULTI-STAGE FITNESS TEST (MSFT)

Equipment needed: tape measure, cones, multi-stage fitness test recording and some speakers to play it through.

1) A recording of a series of timed bleeps is played. You have to run 'shuttles' between two lines, 20 metres apart, starting on the first bleep.

BLEEP!!!

2) Your foot must be on or over the next line when the next bleep sounds.

3) The time between the bleeps gets shorter as you go through the difficulty levels, so you have to run faster.

4) If you miss a bleep, you are allowed two further bleeps to catch up. If you miss three bleeps in a row, the level and number of shuttles completed are noted as your final score.

5) The higher the level and number of shuttles completed, the better your cardiovascular endurance.

*Not that I'm still bitter about it or anything.

The Harvard staircase test — a step too far...

These tests are all for cardiovascular endurance, but some might still be more useful to an athlete than others. E.g. the Cooper swim test is a more useful test of a swimmer's cardiovascular endurance than the Harvard step test.

Q1 State **two** reasons why fitness testing is carried out. [2 marks]

Fitness Testing

Oh my, these tests just keep on coming. A load more for you to learn here, all in pretty coloured boxes...

These Tests are for Muscular Strength and Endurance...

GRIP DYNAMOMETER TEST — STRENGTH

Equipment needed: a dynamometer.

1) A dynamometer is a device used to measure grip strength — the strength in the hand and forearm.

2) You grip as hard as you can for about five seconds and record your reading in kilograms.

3) Usually, you do this three times and take your best score — the higher the score, the stronger your grip.

ONE REP MAX — MAXIMAL STRENGTH

Equipment needed: gym weight equipment.

1) The aim here is to find the heaviest weight you can lift safely using a particular muscle group. The heavier this weight, the stronger the muscle group.

2) Start with a weight you know you can lift. Once you successfully lift it, rest for a few minutes before trying something heavier.

3) Increase the weight you attempt in small steps until you reach a weight with which you can't complete a single lift. The last weight you managed to successfully lift is your one rep max.

ONE-MINUTE SIT-UP AND ONE-MINUTE PRESS-UP TESTS — MUSCULAR ENDURANCE

Equipment needed: stopwatch and a non-slip surface.

1) You just do as many sit-ups or press-ups as you can in a minute.

2) Your result is a number of sit-ups or press-ups per minute — the higher the number, the better your endurance.

3) Sit-ups test your abdominal muscles' endurance, press-ups test the endurance of your upper body.

1001... 1002... 1003

SIT-UP BLEEP TEST — MUSCULAR ENDURANCE

Equipment needed: a metronome (or another way of measuring rate) and a non-slip surface.

1) This is like the one-minute sit-up test, but you have to stick to a set pace of 25 sit-ups a minute.

2) The test is finished either when you fail to do a full sit-up in time twice in a row, or if you manage to keep going for four minutes.

3) You count how many sit-ups you complete. The more you do the better your abdominal muscular endurance.

'Sit-ups' are sometimes called 'abdominal curls'.

The Ruler Drop Test is for Reaction Time...

RULER DROP TEST

Equipment needed: ruler.

1) Get a friend to hold a ruler vertically between your thumb and first finger. The 0 cm mark on the ruler should be in line with the top of your thumb.

2) Your friend drops the ruler — you have to try and catch it as soon as you see it drop.

3) Read off the distance the ruler fell before you managed to catch it.

4) The slower your reactions, the longer it takes you to catch the ruler, so the further up the ruler you'll catch it. This means the smaller the distance recorded, the quicker your reaction time.

'Another French pancake?' — 'No ta, I'm at my one crêpe max'...

To remember which component of fitness is measured by which test, think about the action you're doing. If you're generating lots of force at once, it's testing strength, but if you're repeating a strength action, it's testing endurance.

Q1 State the component of fitness a grip dynamometer test measures.

[1 mark]

Fitness Testing

To remember the names of these fitness tests, just think about the action involved — for speed you sprint, for agility you run, for power you jump and for balance you stand on one leg... like a stork.

Test your Speed and Agility by Sprinting and Running...

30 m SPRINT TEST — SPEED

Equipment needed: stopwatch, tape measure and cones.

1) Run the 30 m as fast as you can and record your time in seconds. The shorter the time (in seconds), the quicker you are.

2) The sprint test can be done over different distances, e.g. 50 m is often used.

ILLINOIS AGILITY RUN TEST — AGILITY

Equipment needed: stopwatch, cones and a tape measure.

1) Set out a course using cones like this.

2) Start lying face down at the start cone. When a start whistle blows, run around the course as fast as you can.

3) The course is set up so you have to constantly change direction. The shorter the time (in seconds) it takes you to complete the course, the more agile you are.

10 m

start   finish
5 m

You can Test your Power by Jumping...

STANDING JUMP TEST

Equipment needed: long jump pit and a tape measure.

1) Place your feet over the edge of the sand pit. Then jump as far forward as possible without a run-up (you can still swing your arms to help). You have to land on both feet.

2) The distance you jump is measured in centimetres — the further you jump the more powerful your leg muscles are.

VERTICAL JUMP TEST

Equipment needed: chalk, tape measure and a wall.

1) Put chalk on your fingertips and stand side-on to a wall.

2) Raise the arm that's nearest the wall and mark the highest point you can reach.

3) Still standing side-on to the wall, jump and mark the wall as high up as you can.

4) Measure between the marks in centimetres. The larger the distance, the more powerful your leg muscles are.

You can test your Balance by, erm... Balancing...

THE STANDING STORK TEST

Cheat!

Equipment needed: stopwatch.

1) Stand on your best leg with your other foot touching your knee and your hands on your hips.

2) Raise your heel so you're standing on your toes and time how long you can hold the position for in seconds. Wobbling is allowed, but the test finishes if your heel touches the ground, or your other foot or hands move.

3) You usually take the best of three times in seconds — the longer your time, the better your balance.

Alaskan agility test — run from the grizzly bear as fast as you can...

Illinois? You take a left at Indiana, if you hit Iowa you've gone too far. With all these US states, this is starting to sound like an old blues song. You'd better do this Practice Question quick, before I start playing the harmonica...

Q1   Describe how to carry out the standing stork test.   [2 marks]

Fitness Testing

The first two tests are for everyone, the rest of the page is only for you if you're doing the Eduqas course.

These tests are for Flexibility and Coordination...

SIT AND REACH TEST — FLEXIBILITY

Equipment needed: ruler or tape measure and a box.

1) This test measures flexibility in the back and lower hamstrings.

2) You sit on the floor with your legs straight out in front of you and a box flat against your feet.

3) You then reach as far forward as you can and an assistant measures the distance reached in centimetres — the further you can reach, the more flexible your back and hamstrings are.

4) The distance reached can be measured in different ways — usually it's how many centimetres past your toes that you manage to reach.

Hermann, I'm afraid you've done one too many sit and reach tests...

ALTERNATE HAND THROW TEST — COORDINATION

Equipment needed: stopwatch, a ball and a wall.

1) This tests hand-eye coordination.

2) Start by standing 2 m away from a wall.

3) Throw a ball underarm from your right hand against the wall and catch it in your left hand — then throw it underarm from your left hand against the wall and catch it in your right hand. You repeat this for 30 seconds and count the number of catches.

4) The more successful catches you make, the better your coordination.

5) This is sometimes called the 'wall toss' or 'wall throw' test.

With the Right Equipment, you can Test Body Composition...

SKINFOLD TEST

Equipment needed: skinfold calipers.

1) The person carrying out the test pinches your skin and underlying fat at different points on your body. They use skinfold calipers to measure the pinched 'fold' in millimetres. Two or three readings are taken at each point, and the average recorded. These average measurements are added together to give a total measurement. This can be put into an equation to estimate your body fat percentage.

2) To get a good estimate the test has to be carried out by someone who's properly trained.

3) The percentage of your total body fat stored under the skin depends on factors like age and gender. You can use different equations to take this into account and make your estimate more accurate.

BODY DENSITY TEST

Equipment needed: scales and specialist underwater weighing equipment.

1) You weigh yourself on land and underwater.

2) Then you use the two measurements and some clever maths to work out your body density and percentage body fat.

This is also called 'hydrostatic weighing'.

Other Measuring Tools can also be used to Monitor Fitness...

As well as the tests of specific components of fitness, there are other ways of measuring fitness and health:

- Monitoring blood pressure. Blood pressure is recorded as two numbers, e.g. 120/80 mmHg. If both these numbers start to decrease, this indicates that your blood pressure is getting lower. This can mean that your fitness and cardiovascular endurance are improving.

- Measuring heart rate (see pages 75 and 77). As you get fitter, and your cardiovascular system improves, your resting heart rate should start to decrease.

- Keeping track of the amount of calories you take in, and how many you use up exercising (see p53).

- Completing health questionnaires (e.g. a PARQ — see p39).

Sit and reach for a biscuit test — now we're talking...

You made it — no more fitness tests to learn. Before you get carried away celebrating, it's Practice Question time.

Q1 Discuss the suitability of the sit and reach test for a kickboxer. [3 marks]

Fitness Testing

You need to understand that these fitness tests are not perfect. But they still give you lots of useful data.

These Fitness Tests have their Limitations

When using any of the fitness tests, you need to consider their limitations:

1) Many of the tests do not test specific sporting actions or the movements involved in an activity.

2) Fitness tests may not tell you how an athlete will actually perform under pressure in a competition.

3) Maximal tests require working at maximum effort — e.g. the one rep max test. The results of these tests will not be accurate if the performer is not motivated to work as hard as they possibly can.

4) Submaximal tests may be used with a formula to predict the maximum performance — the actual maximum is unknown. These formulas can't take into account the differences between individuals, so results can be inaccurate.

5) For some of the tests, you might get better scores just by getting more practice at taking the test, without the relevant component of fitness improving.

Procedures must be followed correctly to make sure the tests are valid and reliable:

- If a test is valid, this means it tests the component of fitness that it's supposed to test.
- If a test is reliable, it will give the same results if it's repeated under the same conditions. So if you see an improvement in the score, it must be because the athlete is doing better at the test.

All these Tests give you Data about your Fitness levels

Fitness testing gives you a number — e.g. a score, a distance, a time, etc. This is data that you can analyse to assess your fitness levels and make decisions.

These numbers are quantitative data (see p73).

1) You can compare your data over time to see how your training is going — e.g. if each week you're recording a bigger distance on the vertical jump test, you know you're increasing your leg power. There's an example of comparing data over time on page 75 — go and have a peek if you like...

2) You can also compare your own performance in a fitness test with average ratings. This can tell you how you rank compared to other people in your age group or gender.

These can be called normative data tables.

3) Each type of fitness test will have a table that you can compare your results with.

The table below shows average ratings for 16 to 19 year-olds taking the grip dynamometer test. Let's say you want to find the rating for an 18-year-old girl who scored 26 kg:

'>' means 'greater than', '<' means 'less than'.

Gender	Excellent	Good	Average	Fair	Poor
Male	> 56 kg	51-56 kg	45-50 kg	39-44 kg	< 39 kg
Female	> 36 kg	31-36 kg	25-30 kg	19-24 kg	< 19 kg

You go down to the correct gender row.

Then read along to find the range of numbers that includes her score.

Finally, go up to see which column this range is in — that gives you the rating.

So, an 18-year-old girl who scored 26 kg on the grip dynamometer test has average grip strength for her gender.

I have a new revision workout for you — number crunches...

Analysing data might be your idea of a living nightmare, but it's key to making sense of all that fitness testing. So, make sure you understand everything on this page. Then do this little Practice Question to check you've got it.

Q1 Sarah scored 5.7 seconds on the 35 m sprint test. Using the data for the 35 m sprint test on the right, which of the following is the correct rating for Sarah?

Rating	Excellent	Good	Average	Fair	Poor
Male (seconds)	<4.80	4.80-5.09	5.10-5.29	5.30-5.60	>5.60
Female (seconds)	<5.30	5.30-5.59	5.60-5.89	5.90-6.20	>6.20

A Excellent   **B** Good   **C** Average   **D** Fair   [1 mark]

Principles of Training

Training isn't about running for as long as possible, or lifting the heaviest weights you can. There's much more to it than that — you need to know how training is matched to different people.

Train to Improve Your Health, Fitness or Performance

1) To improve your health, fitness or performance, you'll need a Personal Exercise Programme (PEP).

2) A PEP is a training programme designed to improve whatever you want it to improve — it could be your general health and fitness, or a particular component of fitness that will improve your performance in a sport or activity.

You will probably have completed a PEP as part of your course...

3) Different training methods involve different types of exercise and are designed to improve different components of fitness.

4) So you need to choose the right training method. Some key factors to consider will be:

What area of your sport or activity you want to improve. You'll need to think about which components of fitness are involved, and which parts of the body too.

For example, you might want to improve your spike in volleyball.

What level of fitness you are currently at — you can use fitness testing to find this out. Some methods of training may be too demanding if you are unfit. With any training method, if you're really unfit you'll want to start easy and build up the intensity slowly.

What facilities and equipment you have access to. Some training methods involve lots of specialist equipment and some will also need lots of indoor space.

SPORT — The Five Principles of Training

To get the most out of your training, you need to follow these five principles:

SPECIFICITY — matching training to the activity and components of fitness to be developed.

Make sure you're training using the muscles and actions you want to improve — e.g. a cyclist would be better off improving their muscular endurance on an exercise bike than a treadmill. You should also match the intensity of your training to the activity you're training for (see p34) and to the individual needs of the performer.

PROGRESSION — gradually increasing the level of training.

This needs to be a gradual process to allow your body time to adapt. If you try to do too much too quickly, you can end up getting injured.

OVERLOAD — the only way to get fitter is to work your body harder than it normally would.

AQA and Edexcel combine these and call it 'progressive overload'.

To overload, you can increase the frequency, intensity, or time spent training (see next page).

REVERSIBILITY — any fitness improvement or body adaptation caused by training will gradually reverse and be lost when you stop training.

Unfortunately, it takes longer to gain fitness than to lose fitness.

TEDIUM — there needs to be variety in your training, otherwise it can become boring.

If you always train in exactly the same way, it'll become boring and you'll lose motivation. Variation in training helps to keep it fresh and interesting.

This principle is called 'variance' if you're doing the Eduqas course.

Delicious Brussels SPROTs — oh, SPORT, that makes more sense...

SPORT, PEP — it's like no one can be bothered to write in whole, actual words any more. Now, time for an EPQ...

Q1   Explain **one** way in which a rower could apply specificity to their training.   [2 marks]

Principles of Training

The best training programmes aren't just thrown together — they have to be <u>carefully</u> planned. Part of this planning is leaving enough time for <u>rest and recovery</u>, so your body has time to <u>adapt</u> to the training.

Training Programmes can be Planned using FITT

<u>F</u>requency, <u>I</u>ntensity and <u>T</u>ime are all part of making sure you <u>overload</u> while you're training.

<u>F</u> = <u>FREQUENCY</u> of training — how <u>often</u> you should exercise.

You can <u>overload</u> by increasing how <u>often</u> you exercise, e.g. <u>gradually increasing</u> the <u>number</u> of training <u>sessions</u>. You need to make sure you leave enough time between sessions to <u>recover</u> though (see below).

This is too intense...

<u>I</u> = <u>INTENSITY</u> of training — how <u>hard</u> you should exercise.

You can <u>overload</u> by <u>gradually increasing</u> the intensity of your exercise — e.g. lifting <u>heavier</u> weights. How <u>intensely</u> you train depends on the <u>type of fitness</u> you want to improve (see next page) and your <u>level of fitness</u> — someone who hasn't trained for a while should start at a <u>low</u> intensity and <u>gradually</u> increase.

I've been hula-hooping for fifty years.

<u>T</u> = <u>TIME</u> spent training — how <u>long</u> you should exercise for.

You can <u>overload</u> by <u>gradually increasing</u> the time you spend on a <u>certain exercise</u> or by increasing the <u>overall time</u> spent exercising — e.g. making training sessions <u>five minutes longer</u> each week.

<u>T</u> = <u>TYPE</u> of training — <u>what exercises</u> and <u>methods of training</u> you should use.

You need to <u>match</u> the <u>type of exercise</u> and <u>method of training</u> to what it is you're <u>training for</u> — e.g. if you want to improve <u>cardiovascular endurance</u>, you need to do exercise that uses <u>lots of muscles</u>, like running or cycling, and you should select an appropriate method of training, e.g. continuous training (see p35). <u>Varying</u> types of exercise also helps <u>stop</u> training becoming <u>boring</u> and reduces stress on <u>tissues</u> and <u>joints</u>.

All training programmes need to be <u>constantly monitored</u> to make sure that the activities are still producing <u>overload</u>. As you get fitter your PEP will need to <u>change</u> to <u>keep</u> improving your fitness.

Your Body Adapts During Rest and Recovery

1) Training makes your body <u>change</u> to <u>cope</u> with the <u>increased</u> exercise. This means you get <u>fitter</u>.

2) These <u>adaptations</u> take place during <u>rest</u> and <u>recovery</u>, so it's vital you allow enough time between training sessions for the body to adapt.

3) It's also important that you allow enough <u>recovery time</u> between workouts to avoid <u>overtraining</u>. <u>Overtraining</u> is when you <u>don't</u> rest enough — it can cause <u>injury</u> by not giving your body enough time to <u>recover</u> from the last training session and <u>repair</u> any damage.

4) When you're training, you need to <u>balance</u> your <u>recovery time</u> with the effects of <u>reversibility</u>.

5) If you rest for <u>too long</u>, you'll <u>lose</u> most of the <u>benefits</u> of having done the training in the first place. If you don't rest enough, you could <u>injure</u> yourself through <u>overtraining</u>.

6) If you get <u>injured</u>, not only have you got to wait for your injury to <u>heal</u>, but thanks to reversibility your <u>fitness</u> will start to decrease while you do. It doesn't seem fair really...

I think I might have overdone it.

Someone's been really creative with these acronyms...

Want to be fit? Use **FITT** — **F**requency, **I**ntensity, **T**ime and **T**ype. And remember that recovery time is part of training too, because your body needs time to adapt and repair itself. Now, time for another Practice Question...

Q1 Describe what is meant by overtraining. Give **one** way that overtraining could decrease fitness. [2 marks]

Training Target Zones

To improve <u>aerobic</u> or <u>anaerobic fitness</u>, you need to be training at the <u>right intensity</u>. To work this out, you have to do some <u>calculations</u> based on your <u>heart rate</u>. If you're doing the OCR course you can skip this page.

Heart Rate — Heartbeats per Minute

1) Your <u>heart rate</u> is the <u>number of times your heart beats per minute (bpm)</u>.

2) When you exercise, your <u>heart rate increases</u> to increase the <u>blood</u> and <u>oxygen supply</u> to your muscles. The <u>harder</u> you work, the more your <u>heart rate</u> will <u>increase</u>.

3) You can find your theoretical <u>maximum heart rate (MHR)</u> by doing: | MHR = 220 – Age |

4) And you can <u>use this value</u> to work out <u>how hard</u> you should work to improve your fitness.

See pages 15-16 for more on how exercise affects your heart rate.

Get your Heart Rate in the Target Zone

Aerobic activity is 'with oxygen' and anaerobic activity is 'without oxygen' — see page 13 for more.

1) To improve your aerobic or anaerobic <u>fitness</u>, you have to exercise at the <u>right intensity</u>.

2) You can do this by making sure that your <u>heart rate</u> is in a <u>target zone</u> — there are different target zones for <u>aerobic</u> and <u>anaerobic training</u>:

> **AEROBIC TARGET ZONE —** 60%-80% of maximum heart rate.

> **ANAEROBIC TARGET ZONE —** 80%-90% of maximum heart rate.

3) The <u>boundaries</u> of the training zones are called <u>training thresholds</u>. If you're a <u>beginner</u>, you should train nearer the <u>lower</u> threshold. <u>Serious</u> athletes train close to the <u>upper</u> threshold.

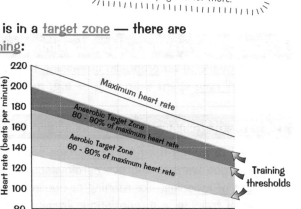

Calculating Target Zones — Example

Let's say you want to work out the <u>aerobic target zone</u> for a <u>20</u>-year-old:

1) First, you calculate their <u>maximum heart rate</u> by subtracting their <u>age</u> from 220 — that's <u>220 – 20 = 200</u>.

2) Next you find the <u>thresholds</u>. Because you're calculating the <u>aerobic</u> target zone, the <u>lower</u> threshold is <u>60%</u> of the maximum heart rate — that's <u>200 × 0.6 = 120</u>. The <u>upper</u> threshold is <u>80%</u> of the maximum heart rate — so <u>200 × 0.8 = 160</u>.

3) So the <u>target zone</u> for aerobic training is <u>between 120 and 160 beats per minute</u>.

For the anaerobic thresholds, you'd use 0.8 and 0.9.

Your Training Intensity Should Suit Your Activity

1) If you want to be good at an <u>aerobic activity</u>, like <u>long-distance running</u>, then you should do a lot of aerobic activity as part of your training. It improves your <u>cardiovascular system</u>.

2) <u>Anaerobic training</u> helps your muscles <u>put up with</u> lactic acid. They also get better at <u>getting rid</u> of it. For <u>anaerobic activity</u> like <u>sprinting</u>, you need to do <u>anaerobic training</u>.

3) In many <u>team sports</u>, like lacrosse, you need to be able to move about <u>continuously</u> (aerobic), as well as needing to have <u>spurts</u> of <u>fast movement</u> (anaerobic). You should have a <u>mix</u> of aerobic and anaerobic activities in your training for these.

Aerobike training

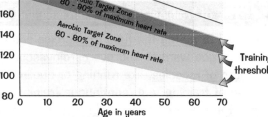

Johnny Depp gets my heart in the target zone...

Make sure you know the percentages that go with aerobic and anaerobic target zones. Keep practising working out different target zones — the more you do it now, the easier it'll be in the exam. Speaking of practice...

Q1 Calculate the lower threshold of the anaerobic training zone for a 35-year-old. [3 marks]

Section Three — Physical Training

Training Methods

Next up, <u>training methods</u>. Remember, you have to match the <u>type</u> of training with what you are training for.

Continuous Training Means No Resting

1) <u>Continuous training</u> involves exercising at a <u>steady</u>, <u>constant rate</u> — doing aerobic activities like <u>running</u> or <u>cycling</u> for at least 20 minutes with <u>no breaks</u>. This is also known as <u>steady-state</u> training.

2) It improves <u>cardiovascular endurance</u> and <u>muscular endurance</u>, and is great for <u>body composition</u> as well.

3) It usually means exercising so that your <u>heart rate</u> is in your <u>aerobic training zone</u> (see p34). This means it's good training for <u>aerobic</u> activities like <u>long-distance running</u>.

4) <u>Overload</u> is achieved by increasing the <u>duration</u>, <u>distance</u>, <u>speed</u> or <u>frequency</u>.

ADVANTAGES:
- It's <u>easy</u> to do — going for a run doesn't require <u>specialist equipment</u>.
- <u>Not resting</u> helps <u>prepare</u> for sports where you have to play for long periods of time <u>without a break</u>.

After six years of continuous training, surely I deserve a rest...

DISADVANTAGES:
- It only involves <u>aerobic</u> activity so doesn't improve <u>anaerobic fitness</u>.
- It can become <u>boring</u> doing one exercise at a constant rate.

Fartlek Training is all about Changes of Speed

1) Fartlek training is a type of continuous training, but it involves changes in the <u>intensity</u> of the exercise over <u>different intervals</u> — e.g. by changing the <u>speed</u> or the <u>terrain</u> (type or steepness of the ground).

For example, part of a fartlek run could be to <u>sprint</u> for <u>10 seconds</u>, then <u>jog</u> for <u>20 seconds</u> (repeated for 4 minutes), followed by <u>running uphill</u> for <u>2 minutes</u>.

2) It's great for <u>cardiovascular endurance</u> and <u>muscular endurance</u> and also helps to improve <u>speed</u>.

3) You can include a <u>mix</u> of <u>aerobic</u> and <u>anaerobic</u> activity, so it's good training for sports that need <u>different paces</u>, like hockey and rugby.

4) <u>Overload</u> is achieved by increasing the <u>times</u> or <u>speeds</u> of each bit, or the terrain <u>difficulty</u> (e.g. running uphill).

ADVANTAGE:
- It's very <u>adaptable</u>, so you can easily <u>tailor</u> training to suit different <u>sports</u> and different <u>levels of fitness</u>.

DISADVANTAGE:
- Frequent changes to intensity can mean that training <u>lacks structure</u> — this makes it easy to <u>skip</u> the hard bits and tough to <u>monitor</u> progress.

Interval Training uses Fixed Patterns of Exercise

1) Interval training uses <u>fixed patterns</u> of periods of <u>high-intensity</u> exercise and either <u>low-intensity</u> exercise or <u>rest</u>. It has a strict <u>structure</u>. For <u>high-intensity interval training (HIIT)</u> you use <u>maximum effort</u> for the high-intensity bits, and an <u>active</u>, <u>low-intensity</u> rest period.

2) By combining high- and low-intensity work, interval training allows you to improve both <u>cardiovascular endurance</u> and <u>anaerobic fitness</u>. The <u>high-intensity</u> periods can also improve <u>speed</u>.

3) It's great training for sports where you have to <u>move continuously</u> (aerobic), then have <u>sudden spurts</u> of <u>fast</u> movement (anaerobic) — like <u>rugby</u> or <u>water polo</u>.

4) To <u>overload</u> you have to increase the <u>proportion</u> of time spent on the <u>high</u>-intensity exercise, or the <u>intensity</u> — e.g. run faster.

ADVANTAGE:
- It's <u>easily adapted</u> to improve <u>aerobic</u> or <u>anaerobic</u> fitness by changing the <u>intensity</u> and <u>length</u> of <u>work</u> and <u>recovery</u> periods.

DISADVANTAGE:
- Interval training is <u>exhausting</u>. This can make it difficult to carry on <u>pushing</u> yourself.

Nige's interval training: run for 1 minute, bathe for 30 minutes, and repeat...

Fartlek training — .... (Add your own joke.)

Once you're done admiring your own wit, there's an Exam Practice Question with your name on it...

Q1 Explain why continuous training is better training for a marathon than for a 100 m sprint. [4 marks]

Training Methods

Resistance training helps you to get stronger. Circuit training lets you do lots of different exercises in one go.

Resistance/Weight Training works on your Muscles

Resistance or weight training means using your muscles against a resistance. You can use weights, elastic ropes or your own body weight (like in a pull-up or press-up) as the resistance.

Improving your strength will also help increase your power.

1) Resistance/weight training can be used to develop both strength and muscular endurance.

2) It's anaerobic training, so is good for improving performance in anaerobic activities like sprinting.

3) Increasing strength/power means you can hit or kick something harder (hockey, football), throw further (javelin, discus), sprint faster, out-muscle opposition (judo), etc.

4) There are two different ways to train — either by moving or by holding a position:

You can train by contracting your muscles to create movement. Each completed movement is called a 'rep' (repetition), and a group of reps is called a 'set'.

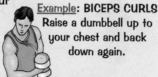

Example: BICEPS CURLS
Raise a dumbbell up to your chest and back down again.

- To increase muscular endurance, you use low weight (below 70% of your one rep max) but a high number of reps. To overload, gradually increase the number of reps.

- To increase strength you use high weight (above 70% of your one rep max) but a low number of reps. To overload, gradually increase the weight — but decrease the reps to avoid injury.

See p28 for how to find your one rep max.

You can train by increasing the tension in a muscle, without changing the muscle's length (so there's no movement).

Example: THE WALL SIT
Sit with your back to the wall and your knees bent at 90° and hold it.

Ouch...

You overload by staying in the position for longer, or holding weights while you're in the position.

The assistant is called a 'spotter'.

ADVANTAGES:
- It's easily adapted to suit different sports — you can focus on the relevant muscles.
- Many of the exercises (press-ups, sit-ups, etc.) require little or no equipment.

DISADVANTAGES:
- It puts muscles under high stress levels, so can leave them very sore afterwards.
- If your weightlifting technique is poor, it can be dangerous. Also, some lifts require an assistant.

Circuit Training Uses Loads of Different Exercises

Each circuit has between 6 and 10 'stations' in it. At each station you do a specific exercise for a set amount of time before moving on to the next station.

1) A circuit's stations can work on aerobic or anaerobic fitness — e.g. star jumps for cardiovascular endurance, tricep dips for strength, shuttle runs for speed, etc.

2) You're allowed a short rest between stations. An active rest, e.g. jogging instead of stopping exercising, will improve cardiovascular endurance.

3) Overload is achieved by doing more repetitions at each station, completing the circuit more quickly, resting less between stations, or by repeating the circuit.

ADVANTAGES:
- Because you design the circuit, you can match circuit training to an individual and any component of fitness — e.g. you can improve muscular endurance, strength, cardiovascular endurance... anything you want really.
- Also, the variety keeps the training interesting.

DISADVANTAGE:
- It takes a long time to set up and requires loads of equipment and space.

I prefer wait training myself — far less strenuous...

Make sure that you understand how resistance/weight training can help with muscular endurance and strength. For endurance do low weight, high reps. For strength do high weight, low reps. Keep saying it over and over...

Q1 Explain how an athlete can train using weights to improve their strength.　　　　[2 marks]

Training Methods

Plyometrics helps make you more powerful. High-altitude training improves your cardiovascular endurance for a short amount of time — you only need to know about this method if you're doing the AQA course.

Plyometric Training Improves Power

Loads of sports require explosive strength and power (see p26), e.g. for fast starts in sprinting, or sports where you need to jump high, like basketball or volleyball. You can train muscular power using plyometrics.

1) When muscles 'contract' to give movement, they either shorten or lengthen.

2) If a muscle lengthens just before it shortens, it can help to generate power. When a muscle gets stretched and lengthens, extra energy is stored in the muscle (like storing energy in an elastic band by stretching it). This extra energy means the muscle can generate a greater force when it shortens.

3) The extra energy doesn't last very long though. So, the quicker your muscles can move between the lengthening and shortening phases, the more powerful the movement will be.

4) Plyometric training improves the speed you can switch between the two phases, so it improves your power. It's anaerobic exercise and often involves jumping.

Depth jumps are a form of plyometric training. They improve the power of your quadriceps and increase how high you can jump. You drop off a box then quickly jump into the air. The first stage lengthens your quadriceps as you land and squat, the second stage shortens them as you jump.

ADVANTAGE:
- It's the only form of training that directly improves your power.

DISADVANTAGE:
- It's very demanding on the muscles used — you need to be very fit to do it, otherwise you'll get injured.

High-Altitude Training Improves Cardiovascular Endurance

1) At high altitude the air pressure is lower. This means you take in less oxygen with each breath.

2) Your body adapts to this by creating more red blood cells, so enough oxygen can still be supplied to the muscles and organs.

Land at high altitude is a long way above sea level.

3) Some athletes take advantage of this by training at high altitude to increase their red blood cell count. This gives them an advantage when they compete at a lower altitude.

4) More red blood cells means a better oxygen supply to the muscles, so it increases a performer's cardiovascular endurance and muscular endurance. This means it suits endurance athletes.

5) Training at high altitude makes it harder to reach the same intensity levels as you could training at a low altitude, so it's not well suited for anaerobic training.

6) The effects of altitude training only last for a few weeks. Once the athlete returns to a lower altitude, the body doesn't need to create extra red blood cells any more.

ADVANTAGE:
- It improves cardiovascular and muscular endurance, which helps endurance athletes perform better.

DISADVANTAGES:
- The effects only last for a short time.
- It can be very expensive to transport athletes to mountainous regions.
- While at high altitude, you can get altitude sickness. This could mean you lose valuable training time recovering.

Altitude training — it's not going to help your fear of heights...

Both the training methods covered on this page are a bit tricky — take your time and make sure you understand what components of fitness they help with, and what type of performer uses them. Time for a Practice Question...

Q1 Justify why a basketball player would train using plyometrics. [3 marks]

Training Methods

Right, last page of training methods... If you're not doing the AQA course you can skip the last part.

Stretching can be used to Improve Flexibility

1) Static stretching is done by gradually stretching a muscle and then holding the position.

2) You hold the stretch at the point where you feel mild discomfort — stretching shouldn't hurt.

3) It's best to do static stretching after a workout, when the muscles are warm.
To improve flexibility, you should hold the stretches for 30 seconds.

4) To avoid injury you should always stretch gradually. This avoids overstretching the muscle.

5) Static stretching can either be active or passive:

- In an ACTIVE static stretch, you use your own muscles to hold the stretch position.

- In a PASSIVE static stretch, you use someone else or a piece of equipment to help you hold the stretch.

6) Dynamic stretching means moving a joint through its range of motion. This should be done during a warm-up as it helps to loosen up muscles, which helps to prevent injury.

> Stretching? No, I always sit like this.

Fitness Classes make Training More Social and More Fun

As well as all those training methods, there's a host of activities and classes that help improve fitness. Classes can also make training a more social experience.

AEROBICS —
This involves doing aerobic exercises to music. It's good for improving cardiovascular endurance, strength and flexibility.

YOGA AND PILATES —
Both yoga and Pilates use a series of exercises and stretches that help increase strength, flexibility and balance.
Both help to prevent injury as well as making you fitter.

> Yoga exercises the whole body, while Pilates focuses more on the core torso muscles, e.g. the abdominals.

BODYPUMP™ — This is a choreographed workout that combines weight training and aerobics. It's good for improving strength, muscular endurance and cardiovascular endurance.

SPINNING® — This is a high-intensity workout using exercise bikes which can be set to different levels of resistance by participants. It's good for improving both your cardiovascular endurance and anaerobic fitness.

> Using any of the training methods covered on the last four pages over a period of time has long-term effects on the body systems. By improving components of fitness, you can improve the performance of the musculo-skeletal and cardio-respiratory systems — see page 17 for the details.
> These changes have a positive effect on both your health and performance in physical activity and sport.

Training needs to be Planned Around when you Compete

Most sportspeople don't compete all year round, so they change their training programmes depending on whether it's before, during or after the competition season:

1) Pre-season (preparation) — a performer makes sure they're ready for the competitive season. The focus is on general fitness and developing the specific components of fitness and skills they need to compete.

2) Competition / playing season (peak) — the performer should be at the peak of their fitness and ability. The focus is on maintaining their current level of fitness, and continuing to develop specific skills to improve their performance. Too much training should be avoided so the performer doesn't become fatigued.

3) Post-season (transition) — once the competition season is over, the performer needs to rest and relax to allow their body to recover. Light aerobic training is done to maintain general fitness.

So many fitness classes to learn — my head is spinning...

That's it — you've made it to the end of training methods, phew. Remember that games players will still need to practise skills and actions that are specific to their sport, as well as improving relevant components of fitness.

Q1 Outline **one** training method a high jumper might use in pre-season. Justify your answer. [3 marks]

Preventing Injuries

With any physical activity there's always a risk of injury. You need to know how to make it as safe as possible.

PARQ — Physical Activity Readiness Questionnaire

1) PARQs are made up of 'yes or no' questions, designed to assess whether it's safe for you to increase your physical activity.

2) It's a good idea to fill one in before you start a training programme.

3) If you answer yes to any of the questions, you need to visit your doctor to make sure it's safe first. This could also lead to changes in the programme to make sure it's safe for you to participate.

PARQ	Yes	No
• Have you ever been diagnosed with a heart problem?	☐	☐
• Are you currently being prescribed any medication?	☐	☐
• Do you have any problems with your joints?	☐	☐

Before you Exercise do these Three Things...

CHECK EQUIPMENT/FACILITIES

• Use the right equipment — and check it's not damaged and is in good condition.

• Check for possible dangers in the area you're going to be exercising in — e.g. glass hidden in the grass on a football pitch, slippery patches caused by bad weather on a running track, loose or slippery tiles around a swimming pool.

STRUCTURE TRAINING CORRECTLY

• Apply the Principles of Training (see p32-33).

• This means planning your training correctly — you need to allow time for rest and recovery, otherwise you can get overuse injuries. Also, make sure the intensity of exercise matches your level of fitness.

WARM UP

• See the next page for how to warm up properly...

During Exercise do these Six Things...

USE THE CORRECT CLOTHING/EQUIPMENT

• Make sure you're not wearing anything that could get caught (e.g. jewellery, watches).

• Wear suitable footwear — e.g. wearing studded football boots or spiked running shoes can make you less likely to slip and injure yourself.

• Use protective clothing/equipment where appropriate — e.g. gumshields, cycling helmets.

USE THE CORRECT TECHNIQUE

• Make sure that you use the correct technique — e.g. lifting weights properly, or stretching in the right way.

• Also, make sure that you use the right technique for moving and carrying equipment.

COMPETE AT THE APPROPRIATE LEVEL

• You should exercise with people at a similar level to yourself, so you don't overdo it — e.g. join a running club who run at a similar pace to yourself.

• You need to compete in the right age range too — e.g. a 10-year-old shouldn't play rugby with adults.

MAINTAIN HYDRATION

• Drink plenty of water to replace the water lost while exercising. This stops you becoming dehydrated (see p50).

USE TAPING AND BRACING

• You can use special tape or an elastic brace to support joints.

• This restricts the range of movement at a joint, which helps to prevent sprains (see p41).

• It's important that this is done for joints that have been recently injured, to help avoid another injury.

PLAY BY THE RULES

• Know and follow the rules. Some rules are there to help stop injuries — e.g. giving yellow cards for bad tackles in football.

• Use officials (e.g. a referee) to ensure there's fair play and the rules are followed.

All this talk of injuries is making my brain hurt...

You need to be able to apply these ways of preventing injury to different activities, so think about the actions involved and also where the activity takes place. Now, time for an Exam Practice Question to check you've got it.

Q1 Explain one way a referee can help rugby players to avoid injury during a match. [1 mark]

Preventing Injuries

Warming up before exercise and cooling down afterwards are vital — they have tons of benefits.

What you do After you Exercise is Important too...

COOL DOWN

• See below for how to cool down...

EAT AND REHYDRATE

• Exercising will have used up a lot of the energy stored in your body. You need to replenish this energy, e.g. by eating carbohydrates (see p49).

• You'll also need to drink plenty of water to rehydrate (see p50).

LEAVE ENOUGH RECOVERY TIME

• You need to leave enough time for your body to repair and rebuild after exercise. If you don't you could end up overtraining (see p33).

ICE BATHS/MASSAGE

• Some athletes will take ice baths or get sports massages following exercise. These may help to prevent delayed onset of muscle soreness (DOMS).

Before Exercise you should always Warm Up...

A warm-up gets your body ready for exercise by gradually increasing your work rate. It should involve:

1) Raising your pulse — light exercise increases your heart rate and gets blood flowing to the muscles.
   • This raises your body temperature and warms up muscles, ligaments and tendons so they can move more freely and are less likely to get injured. Warmer muscles can also contract more quickly.
   • It also helps to ease your body into exercising by gradually increasing the exercise intensity, and it increases the oxygen supply to the muscles.

2) Stretching and mobility exercises — this increases flexibility at your joints. It should focus on the muscles and movements you will use in the activity — e.g. shoulder circles before playing tennis.
   • This helps increase the range of movement of your muscles and joints, which will help you perform better and avoid injury. It's best to use dynamic stretches (see p38).

3) Practice actions — e.g. practice shots in netball, throwing and catching in rounders, etc.
   • This prepares the muscles that will be used in the activity, so they perform better.
   • It also helps with your mental preparation, as it focuses you on the activity and gets you "in the zone".

You could also use mental preparation techniques so you're calm, confident and focused (see page 60).

...And Afterwards you should Cool Down

A cool-down gets your body back to normal after exercise by gradually decreasing the intensity of work to control your return to resting levels. It should involve:

1) Gentle exercise like jogging to keep the heart and lungs working harder than normal. You should gradually reduce the intensity of this exercise so that your heart rate, breathing rate and body temperature decrease gradually.
   • This means you can continue taking in more oxygen to help get rid of the lactic acid and other waste products in your muscles (repaying the oxygen debt — see p14). It also helps you to remove the extra carbon dioxide in your blood.
   • It keeps the blood flowing back from the muscles, so stops blood pooling in the legs and arms — blood pooling can cause dizziness and even fainting.

2) Stretching the muscles that have been used in the activity to speed up recovery and improve flexibility.
   • Stretching while the muscles are warm helps to improve flexibility — in particular using static or PNF stretches. PNF stretches involve contracting the muscle you are stretching to increase mobility gains.
   • It may also help to prevent delayed onset of muscle soreness (DOMS).

Arrrrrghhhhhhhhghghghghhhh — I thought you said 'A nice bath'...

Warming up is especially important for more intense, anaerobic activities, where it's easy to get an injury.

Q1 Evaluate the importance of a pre-match warm-up in helping a hockey player to avoid injury. [9 marks]

Injuries and Treatment

As my grandma used to say, 'It's all <u>fun and games</u> until someone gets <u>hurt</u>.' And she would know — she's a <u>prize-winning cage-fighter</u>... Only read these next <u>two pages</u> about <u>injuries</u> if you're doing the <u>Edexcel</u> course.

Soft Tissues can get Stretched, Ripped and Torn

Soft tissues are <u>skin</u>, <u>muscles</u>, <u>tendons</u> and <u>ligaments</u>. Basically, all the bits of you that <u>aren't bone</u>...

Damage to the Skin is Common in Sport

1) <u>Grazes</u>, <u>blisters</u> and <u>chafing</u> are all types of <u>abrasion</u>. They can <u>break</u> the skin and cause <u>bleeding</u>.

2) <u>Cuts</u> also damage the skin and cause bleeding. A <u>deep</u> cut will damage the tissue <u>beneath</u> the skin as well. Deep cuts like this will require <u>medical attention</u>.

3) Injuries to the skin can occur in most physical activities, although they're especially common in <u>full-contact sports</u> like <u>rugby</u> or <u>boxing</u>.

Strains are Tears in Muscles or Tendons

1) <u>Strained</u> (pulled) muscles and tendons are <u>tears</u> in the tissue. They're often caused by sudden <u>overstretching</u>.

2) Pulled <u>hamstrings</u> and <u>calf muscles</u> are common injuries in sports like football and cricket, where you use <u>sudden bursts</u> of speed.

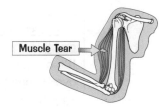

Muscle Tear

Sprains are Damage to Ligaments

1) <u>Sprains</u> are <u>joint</u> injuries where the <u>ligament</u> has been stretched or torn, usually because of violent twisting.

2) These types of injuries are common in sports where players have to <u>change direction quickly</u>, like football and basketball.

See page 4 for more about <u>tendons</u> and <u>ligaments</u>.

Some Injuries are Caused by Continuous Stress...

<u>Continuous stress</u> on part of the body over a <u>long</u> period of time can cause all sorts of problems:

1) Tennis players can develop <u>tennis elbow</u> — painful inflammation of tendons in the elbow due to overuse of certain arm muscles.

2) Golfers get a similar injury called, wait for it... <u>golfer's elbow</u>.

3) You're more at risk of this type of injury if you <u>train too hard</u> or <u>don't rest</u> enough between training sessions.

4) As these are injuries to <u>tendons</u>, they are also types of <u>soft-tissue injury</u>.

Ouch...

...others by Sudden Stress

1) <u>Cartilage</u> can be damaged by sudden movements.

2) E.g. the cartilage of the <u>knee</u> can be <u>torn</u> by a violent <u>impact</u> or <u>twisting</u> motion.

3) <u>Joints</u> can get <u>dislocated</u> as well.

4) The bone is pulled out of its normal position — again, it's <u>twisting</u> that usually does it.

5) This can damage the ligaments, muscles and tendons <u>around</u> the joint too.

This type of injury is common in sports like football and rugby.

See page 4 for more about <u>cartilage</u>.

Dislocated shoulder
Humerus pulled out of joint.

Sprains, Strains and Automobiles...

It's easy to get sprains and strains mixed up. So, write down 'a strain is a muscle or tendon injury' over and over until it's lodged nice and firmly in your brain. And now, free cake... (Not really, just another Exam Practice Question.)

Q1 Name the soft tissue damaged in a sprain. [1 mark]

Injuries and Treatment

My grandma isn't really a cage-fighter — that was a lie. She does make a mean rice pudding though. You can treat injuries using the RICE method — Rest, Ice, Compression and Elevation. Neat huh?

Broken Bones are Called Fractures

1) A fracture is a break in a bone. It's usually accompanied by bruising and swelling.

2) This is because a fracture also damages the blood vessels in or around the bone.

3) It'll also cause a lot of pain because of the damaged nerves inside the bone.

4) There are four types of fracture you need to know:

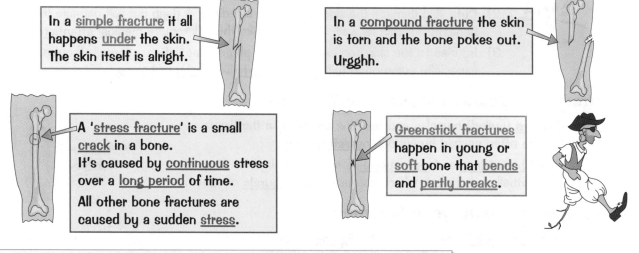

In a simple fracture it all happens under the skin. The skin itself is alright.

In a compound fracture the skin is torn and the bone pokes out. Urgghh.

A 'stress fracture' is a small crack in a bone.
It's caused by continuous stress over a long period of time.
All other bone fractures are caused by a sudden stress.

Greenstick fractures happen in young or soft bone that bends and partly breaks.

Concussion is Caused by a Blow to the Head

1) A concussion is a mild brain injury caused by a nasty blow to the head.

2) The symptoms of concussion are: disorientation, memory loss and possibly loss of consciousness.

3) If someone with concussion is unconscious, check they've not injured their neck or spine, then place them in the recovery position (with the head tilted so the airway won't be blocked by the tongue or by vomit) and get an ambulance. If they're conscious, keep them under observation for at least 48 hours.

Use the RICE Method to Treat Injuries

R   REST ➡ Stop immediately and rest the injury — if you carry on, you'll make it worse.

I   ICE ➡ Apply ice to the injury. This makes the blood vessels contract to reduce internal bleeding and swelling.

C   COMPRESSION ➡ Bandaging the injury will also help reduce swelling. But don't make it so tight that you stop the blood circulating altogether.

E   ELEVATION ➡ Support the limb at a raised level (i.e. above the heart). The flow of blood reduces because it has to flow against gravity.

I've got the rice.

What are they doing?

The RICE method is a good treatment for joint and muscle injuries like sprains or strains. It reduces pain, swelling and bruising. But, if there's an injury to the neck or spine, it's best not to move the person.

If the RICE treatment doesn't work, try the noodles...

What a pair of really nasty pages. With all the bones, and the breaking... Lots of stuff to know here — no way around it I'm afraid, so get memorising. Then it's time for another Exam Practice Question methinks.

Q1   Explain how to treat a sprained ankle.   [2 marks]

Performance-Enhancing Drugs

Some people <u>cheat</u> by taking <u>drugs</u>. Drugs can help them <u>perform better</u>, but they can also cause serious <u>health problems</u>. You need to know the <u>positive</u> and <u>negative</u> effects of these drugs on the performer...

Performance-Enhancing Drugs can Improve Performance

1) Some performers use drugs to <u>improve</u> their performance and be more <u>successful</u> in their sport, which can lead to <u>wealth</u> and <u>fame</u>. Some performers also claim they use drugs to <u>level the playing field</u> — if other competitors use drugs, you're at a disadvantage unless you use them too.

2) The use of these drugs in sport is usually <u>banned</u>, and they can have <u>nasty side effects</u>.

3) Unfortunately, some performers still <u>break the rules</u> by taking them anyway — even with the <u>risks</u> to their <u>health</u> and <u>reputation</u> and to the <u>reputation</u> and <u>credibility</u> of their <u>sport</u> if they're caught. These are the drugs you need to know about:

See p70 for more about punishments for using drugs.

BETA BLOCKERS

- <u>Reduce heart rate</u>, <u>muscle tension</u>, <u>blood pressure</u> and the <u>effect of adrenaline</u>. This <u>steadies shaking hands</u>, which improves <u>fine motor skills</u>, and has a <u>calming</u>, <u>relaxing</u> effect.

But...
- They can cause <u>nausea</u>, <u>weakness</u>, <u>low blood pressure</u>, <u>cramp</u> and <u>heart failure</u>.
- They're <u>banned</u> in some sports and if allowed must be <u>prescribed</u> by a <u>medical professional</u>.

DIURETICS

- Increase the amount you <u>urinate</u>, causing <u>weight loss</u> — which may be important if you're competing in a certain <u>weight division</u>.
- Can <u>mask traces</u> of other drugs in the body.

But...
- They can cause <u>cramp</u>, <u>dehydration</u>, <u>loss of salts</u>, <u>muscle weakness</u> and <u>heart damage</u>.

NARCOTIC ANALGESICS

- <u>Kill pain</u> — so injuries and fatigue, e.g. from overtraining, don't affect performance and training so much.

But...
- They're <u>addictive</u>, with unpleasant <u>withdrawal symptoms</u>.
- Feeling less pain can make an athlete train <u>too hard</u>, causing <u>overtraining</u>.
- They can lead to <u>constipation</u> and <u>low blood pressure</u>.

STIMULANTS

- Affect the <u>central nervous system</u> (the bits of your brain and spine that control your <u>reactions</u>).
- They can <u>increase mental</u> and <u>physical alertness</u>.

But...
- They can lead to <u>high blood pressure</u>, <u>heart</u> and <u>liver problems</u>, and <u>strokes</u>.
- They're <u>addictive</u>.

ANABOLIC STEROIDS (AGENTS)

- Mimic the male sex hormone <u>testosterone</u>.
- Testosterone <u>increases</u> your <u>bone</u> and <u>muscle growth</u> (so you can get bigger and stronger). It can also make you more <u>aggressive</u>.

But...
- They can cause <u>high blood pressure</u>, <u>heart disease</u> and <u>infertility</u>, and can increase the risk of developing <u>cancer</u>.
- Women may grow <u>facial</u> and <u>body hair</u>, and their voice may <u>deepen</u>.

PEPTIDE HORMONES

- Cause the production of other hormones — <u>similar</u> to anabolic steroids.
- <u>EPO</u> (Erythropoietin) is a peptide hormone that causes the body to produce more red blood cells.
- <u>GH</u> (Growth Hormones) are peptide hormones that make the body build more muscle.

But...
- They can cause <u>strokes</u> and <u>heart problems</u>. GH can also cause <u>abnormal growth</u> and <u>diabetes</u>.

Blood Doping is Banned

You can improve your performance by <u>increasing</u> the number of <u>red blood cells</u> in your bloodstream to increase the <u>oxygen supply</u> to your muscles. Blood doping is a form of <u>cheating</u> that increases a performer's number of red blood cells <u>unfairly</u>. It can be done in one of two ways:

1) Before a competition a performer can be <u>injected</u> with red blood cells. Possible side effects of injecting red blood cells include <u>allergic reactions</u>, <u>kidney damage</u>, <u>blood thickening</u>, <u>blocked blood vessels (embolism)</u> and <u>increased risk of heart attack</u>. If the blood is from someone else there's also the risk of catching <u>viruses</u> like **HIV**.

2) Performers can also take <u>EPO</u> to increase their red blood cell count (see peptide hormones above).

Cheating — it's just not worth it...

A trick for remembering these: think BADSNAP — (<u>B</u>eta blockers, <u>A</u>nabolic steroids, <u>D</u>iuretics, <u>S</u>timulants, <u>N</u>arcotic <u>A</u>nalgesics, <u>P</u>eptide hormones). Now, guess what? That's right, Exam Practice Question time...

Q1 Identify one performance-enhancing drug that might benefit an archer. Explain your choice. [2 marks]

Revision Questions for Section Three

So, it turns out there's more to <u>physical training</u> than montages, slow motion and cheesy power ballads...

- Try these questions and <u>tick off each one</u> when you <u>get it right</u>.
- When you've done <u>all the questions</u> for a topic and are <u>completely happy</u> with it, tick off the topic.
- The answers can all be found by <u>looking back over pages 22 to 43</u>.

Health and Fitness (p22)

1) Write a definition of fitness.
2) Write a definition of performance.
3) Give two ways that exercise can help keep you healthy.

Components of Fitness (p23-26)

4) What is cardiovascular endurance?
5) Give an example of a sport where muscular endurance is important.
6) Define flexibility. Give one benefit of increased flexibility for an athlete.
7) Describe coordination. How does having good coordination help a sprinter?
8) What is power? Give an example of when power would be needed in golf.

Fitness Testing (p27-31)

9) Describe the Harvard step test. Which component of fitness does it measure?
10) Outline a fitness test that measures: a) speed, b) power, c) muscular endurance, d) agility.
11) Which component of fitness does the sit and reach test measure? What units are the results in?
12) What is meant by a reliable fitness test?

Training (p32-38)

13) Name five important principles of training.
14) Give three ways that overload can be achieved in training.
15) What are the four principles of FITT?
16) Describe how to calculate your anaerobic target zone.
17) Does continuous training improve anaerobic fitness?
18) Describe the fartlek training method. Give an advantage and a disadvantage.
19) How is overload achieved in circuit training?
20) Which component of fitness does plyometric training improve?
21) Describe common differences in pre-season and playing-season training programmes.

Injuries and Treatment (p39-42)

22) What does PARQ stand for? Should it be used before or after a training programme?
23) Outline two benefits of warming up and two benefits of cooling down.
24) Name the soft tissue damaged in: a) an abrasion, b) a sprain, c) a strain.
25) Give three symptoms of a concussion.
26) What does RICE stand for? Give two types of injury that can be treated with the RICE method.

Performance-Enhancing Drugs (p43)

27) Describe the positive and negative effects of: a) beta blockers, b) diuretics, c) stimulants.
28) Outline two methods of blood doping. What are the health risks involved in each method?

Health, Fitness and Well-being

Regular physical activity helps you to be healthy by improving your physical, emotional and social health and well-being. First up, the obvious one — exercise helps keep you physically healthy...

If your Body Works Well, you are Physically Healthy

1) Physical health and well-being is an important part of being healthy and happy.

2) Taking part in sport or other physical activities has loads of physical benefits.

See p17 for more about how exercise benefits your body systems.

PHYSICAL HEALTH AND WELL-BEING:

1) Your body's organs, e.g. the heart, and systems, e.g. the cardiovascular system, are working well.

2) You're not suffering from any illnesses, diseases or injuries.

3) You're strong and fit enough to easily do everyday activities.

2) These positive effects on the body reduce the risk of obesity and other long-term health problems (see below). Stronger muscles and more flexible joints can make injury less likely and improve your posture. Avoiding injury also means you can continue training.

1) By exercising you can improve components of fitness (see p23-26), which benefits your physical health:

• Aerobic exercise improves your cardiovascular endurance — your heart, blood vessels and lungs work more efficiently, so you can exercise more intensely and for longer. Your blood pressure also decreases.

• Exercise can benefit your musculo-skeletal system — muscles and bones get stronger, and joints more flexible.

• Exercise can improve body composition — you can attain a healthy weight, which reduces strain on your body.

3) Physical activity makes you stronger and fitter — so everyday tasks like climbing stairs and lifting shopping are easier. This can help your emotional well-being too (see next page). It's not all good though — overtraining (see p33) can have a negative effect on your health.

Novelty size veggies ltd.

Now that's what I call shoplifting.

Exercise Reduces Risks to Long-Term Health

Regular physical activity can help reduce the risks of you getting certain diseases. For example:

1) Regular aerobic exercise helps prevent high blood pressure by keeping your heart strong and arteries elastic, and helping to remove cholesterol from artery walls.

2) This means blood can flow easily round the body, which reduces the risk of coronary heart disease (CHD), strokes and damage to your arteries.

Exercise increases levels of high density lipoprotein (HDL). HDL helps to remove cholesterol from the arteries.

I'm not sure we've got this quite right...

Weight-bearing exercise can help to prevent osteoporosis — a disease where your bones become fragile. As you get older, the risk of osteoporosis increases. Weight-bearing exercise, where your legs and feet support your whole body weight (like aerobics or running), helps to strengthen your bones by increasing bone density.

Regular exercise helps prevent obesity. Exercise uses up energy, meaning that your body doesn't store it as fat (see p48).

Type-2 diabetes is a disease that gives you a high blood sugar level. Your blood sugar level is controlled by a hormone called insulin. If you have diabetes, this means you don't have enough insulin or your body's cells aren't reacting to insulin properly (they're insulin-resistant).

Regular exercise helps you avoid diabetes in two ways:

1) Regular exercise helps you maintain a healthy weight. This makes you far less likely to get diabetes.

2) Regular exercise helps improve how sensitive to insulin your cells are. This means you are less likely to become insulin-resistant.

Middle-aged and older adults have a far higher risk of diabetes, so exercise is a great way for them to lower that risk.

All these benefits of exercise and I'm sitting around writing jokes...

Remember that health and fitness are defined back on p22 — flick back and take a look if you need a little reminder... And now, here's an Exam Practice Question for you, because I know how much you love 'em.

Q1   Explain **one** way that regular exercise helps to prevent type-2 diabetes.   [2 marks]

Health, Fitness and Well-being

As well as making you into a Schwarzenegger-like picture of physical health, exercise is great for your emotional and social health. You need to be able to give examples of how it helps.

Emotional Health is about how you Feel

1) Being healthy is more than just having a body that works well — you also have to take into account how you feel. Your emotional health and well-being is based on how you feel about yourself and how you respond to different situations.

Emotional health can also be called 'psychological health'.

2) Taking part in physical activity and sport can have emotional benefits:

I'm amazing...

EMOTIONAL HEALTH AND WELL-BEING:

1) You feel content and confident in yourself.

2) You are able to manage your emotions and cope with challenges.

3) You don't have too much stress or anxiety.

4) You're not suffering from any mental illnesses.

1) Physical activity can increase your self-esteem (your opinion of yourself) and confidence and generally make you feel better about yourself, e.g. if you feel you've achieved something. Seeing improvements in your physical health, e.g. losing weight or gaining strength, can improve your self-image.

2) Competing against others (or yourself) can improve your ability to deal with pressure and manage emotions, e.g. by giving you a controlled way to channel your aggression. It's also a great way for young children to learn these skills.

3) Doing physical activity can help relieve stress and tension by taking your mind off whatever's worrying you and by making you feel happier. This helps prevent stress-related illnesses.

4) When you do physical activity, the level of endorphins in your brain increases. Endorphins help you to feel good, which can reduce your risk of mental illnesses like depression. Exercise also increases the level of serotonin in your brain. This may help reduce the risk of mental illness, as low levels of serotonin are connected with depression.

Stressed? Me? Don't be ridiculous.

Social Health is about how you Relate to Society

1) Your social health and well-being is about how you interact with others and form relationships.

2) There can be plenty of social benefits from doing physical activity and sport:

SOCIAL HEALTH AND WELL-BEING:

1) You have friends.

2) You believe you have some worth in society.

3) You have food, clothing and shelter.

1) Doing physical activity can help you make friends with people of different ages and backgrounds. For example, some elderly folk may have fewer opportunities to socialise, so sport can be a great way to make new friends. It's also a great way of socialising with your current friends.

2) By taking part in team activities like football, you have to practise teamwork — how to cooperate and work with other people. These skills are useful in all walks of life and can help you to be successful, which will increase your sense of worth. Being part of a team can help you to feel more involved in society as a whole.

Ricky made lots of new friends at the local boxing gym.

3) For many people, physical activity probably won't put a roof over their heads. But the skills you learn through exercise and sport can help you succeed at work as well as at the gym or on the playing field. Being physically fit can also help if your job involves manual labour or being on your feet all day.

Pumping iron with a grin on your face — serotonin' up...

These benefits are less obvious than those on the last page — especially the social health ones. But take your time and jot them down again and again until you've got them all stored in your head. Then try this Practice Question...

Q1 Give **two** emotional health benefits of exercise.   [2 marks]

Lifestyle Choices

Lifestyle choices — like how you eat and drink, whether or not you smoke and how much sleep you get — will all have a knock-on effect on your fitness and your health. So, choose wisely and read this whole page.

Key Lifestyle Choices — Think DRAW

There are four areas of lifestyle choices that you need to know — Diet, Recreational drugs, Activity level and your Work/rest/sleep balance. The first letters spell DRAW, which is handy for remembering them.

Pages 49-51 cover diet in more depth...

1) Diet

1) A balanced diet helps support a healthy lifestyle. Your body needs the right nutrients to work well — and these nutrients provide energy so you can exercise and improve your health.

2) A diet that's too high in some fats, sugar or salt can have negative effects on your health and can increase the risk of obesity. Too much salt can also increase blood pressure. This increases the risk of strokes and heart disease.

3) Not eating enough is also dangerous and can lead to malnutrition — this is where the body does not have enough nutrients to maintain good health.

2) Recreational Drugs — Alcohol and Nicotine

You know, your smoking really irritates me.

ALCOHOL

1) Alcohol affects your coordination, speech and judgement. Your reaction time gets slower.

2) Drinking large amounts often causes an increase in blood pressure, so increases your risk of stroke and heart disease.

3) Eventually, heavy drinking will damage your liver, heart, muscles, brain and the digestive and immune systems.

SMOKING

1) The chemicals in cigarette smoke cause damage to cells in the lungs and small hairs in your windpipe called cilia.

2) This increases the risk of getting infections, which can lead to bronchitis (inflammation of the major airways) or pneumonia (inflammation deep in the lungs).

3) The damage to alveoli causes them to lose their shape, so they work less efficiently. This is called emphysema.

4) The damage to your lungs can also cause lung cancer.

5) Tobacco also contains the addictive drug nicotine, which raises your heart rate and blood pressure.

Any damage to the lungs makes breathing more difficult, so affects fitness and performance.

3) Activity Level

To be healthy, you need to be active. See p45-46 for all the positive effects of physical activity and how it can reduce health risks. There's more about the impact of an inactive lifestyle on the next page.

To improve health and fitness, you can design a personal exercise programme (PEP — see p32). Your PEP should be tailored to your individual needs and monitored so you get the benefits you want.

4) Work/Rest/Sleep Balance

1) You need to make time to rest and relax after work to help relieve any stress or anxiety you're feeling.

2) If you're feeling stressed, your blood pressure increases. If this continues over a long period of time, it increases the risk of heart disease and strokes.

3) Stress and anxiety also affects your emotional well-being. They can cause insomnia (trouble sleeping) and depression.

4) Sleep is vital for your body as it allows it to rest and recover after a day's work.

5) Lack of sleep affects your ability to concentrate. It also makes you uncoordinated and your muscles become fatigued quicker. In the long term it can lead to anxiety and depression.

Jim's started smoking — that boy's getting cilia and cilia...

Some of the topics on this page are covered in more detail on other pages. Not the stuff about smoking, drinking and work/rest/sleep balance though, so make sure you learn that good and proper. Exam Practice Question time...

Q1 Explain **one** way that smoking can have a negative impact on health. [3 marks]

Sedentary Lifestyle

<u>Couch potatoes</u> be warned — sitting still all day <u>isn't</u> good for you. Apart from sitting still all day <u>revising</u> that is...

A Sedentary Lifestyle has Many Long-term Health Risks

Basically, if you have a <u>sedentary lifestyle</u>, it means you don't exercise <u>enough</u>:

> A <u>sedentary lifestyle</u> is one where there is <u>little, irregular</u> or <u>no physical activity</u>.

1) If you aren't <u>active</u> enough, you don't use up <u>all</u> the energy you get from <u>food</u>. Any excess energy is stored as <u>fat</u>, which increases your risk of becoming <u>overweight</u>, <u>overfat</u> or even <u>obese</u>.

> Being OVERWEIGHT means weighing <u>more</u> than is <u>normal</u>.

> Being OVERFAT means having more <u>body fat</u> than you should.

> Being OBESE means having <u>a lot</u> more <u>body fat</u> than you should.

2) Being <u>overfat</u> (or <u>obese</u>) puts more <u>strain</u> on your <u>cardiovascular</u> system and decreases <u>cardiovascular endurance</u>. Increased body fat can also lead to <u>high cholesterol</u> and <u>fatty deposits</u> in the <u>arteries</u>, making it <u>harder</u> for the heart to pump blood. This <u>increases blood pressure</u> and the risk of <u>strokes</u> and <u>coronary heart disease</u>.

If you're inactive but skinny, you're still at risk of health problems.

3) You are also more likely to develop <u>type-2 diabetes</u> if you are obese (see **p45**), and are more at risk of getting certain <u>cancers</u>.

4) Being overweight <u>decreases flexibility</u>, <u>speed</u> and <u>agility</u>, so affects your <u>performance</u> too.

5) A sedentary lifestyle also affects the <u>musculo-skeletal system</u>. By not exercising enough, the body loses <u>muscle tone</u>, <u>joints</u> get <u>stiffer</u> and <u>bones</u> become <u>weaker</u> — increasing the risk of <u>osteoporosis</u>. Being overweight puts <u>strain</u> on your <u>back</u> and <u>joints</u>. This can lead to <u>bad posture</u> and <u>joint damage</u>.

6) A sedentary lifestyle and obesity can cause <u>lethargy</u> (always feeling tired) and <u>poor sleep</u>, and lead to <u>emotional health problems</u> like <u>low confidence</u> and <u>self-esteem</u>, <u>poor body image</u> and <u>depression</u>. These problems can affect <u>social health</u> if it becomes hard to go out and <u>socialise</u> with others.

Data About Health Issues can be Plotted as a Graph

You can <u>analyse</u> data on health issues to understand how things are <u>changing over time</u>. This allows you to spot <u>trends</u> and make predictions about the <u>future</u>.

Here's an example of the kind of graph you could get in your <u>exam</u>:

NB: You will <u>not</u> be allowed a crystal ball in the exam.

- You can either <u>describe</u> what's happening <u>over time</u> (see <u>1</u>), or at certain <u>points in time</u> (see <u>2</u> and <u>3</u>).
- Be <u>specific</u> — give the <u>exact</u> dates for the part of the graph you're describing — e.g. 'in 2010', 'from 1993 to 2009'.
- Make sure you say <u>enough</u> to get <u>all</u> the <u>marks</u>.

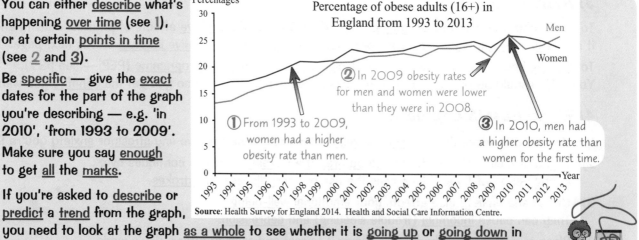

Percentage of obese adults (16+) in England from 1993 to 2013

① From 1993 to 2009, women had a higher obesity rate than men.

② In 2009 obesity rates for men and women were lower than they were in 2008.

③ In 2010, men had a higher obesity rate than women for the first time.

Source: Health Survey for England 2014. Health and Social Care Information Centre.

- If you're asked to <u>describe</u> or <u>predict</u> a <u>trend</u> from the graph, you need to look at the graph <u>as a whole</u> to see whether it is <u>going up</u> or <u>going down</u> in the <u>long term</u>. Then you need to predict whether this is likely to <u>continue</u>. E.g. in the graph above, there's a general <u>upward trend</u> in obesity rates for men and women. This trend looks like it will <u>continue</u> for <u>men</u>, but rates for <u>women</u> have started <u>decreasing</u>.

This trend is out of control...

Sedentary? Not me — I get up and put the kettle on sometimes...

Data questions pop up everywhere, so make sure you really get the hang of graphs. Now, Practice Question time.

Q1 Give **two** long-term health risks that are increased by a sedentary lifestyle. [2 marks]

Diet, Nutrition and Performance

Eating for sport ain't all hot-dog guzzling contests and chilli cook-offs... You need to know how your diet can affect your performance and how different activities need different nutrients at different times.

Different Types of Physical Activity Require Different Nutrients

1) The type of physical activity you are doing affects the balance of nutrients you need.

2) If your activity involves long periods of continuous exercise, like competing in a triathlon, you need a diet rich in carbohydrates. This is because carbohydrates provide plenty of energy that is easily available for your muscles. Fat is also an important energy source for endurance athletes as it can provide energy for low to moderate intensity exercise when supplies of carbohydrates are running low.

3) If your activity involves gaining muscle bulk — like sprinting or weightlifting, you need a diet rich in protein in order to build and repair your muscles.

4) Carrying around extra weight as fat can affect performance. So, for many physical activities, you will want a diet that helps keep body fat low.

5) Hydration (the body having the right amount of water) is really important when you're exercising (see p50). It's especially important to take in water during activities where you sweat a lot and have an increased breathing rate for a long period of time.

Organise Your Meals Around Activities

It's not just what you eat — when you eat is really important too if you want to perform well.

1) You should drink to replace lost fluid both during and after an activity (see previous page).

2) You shouldn't eat during exercise, or for a couple of hours before, due to blood shunting:

> When you exercise, blood is redistributed around the body to increase the supply of oxygen to your muscles (see p15).
>
> This means blood is taken away from your digestive system — which makes it harder for you to digest food, so you end up feeling sick.

3) After exercise, within an hour, you should start eating to replace used energy.

Endurance Athletes use Carbohydrate Loading Before Events

1) Endurance athletes will often increase their carbohydrate intake a few days before an event.

2) They'll also take it easy in training just before the event, so that most of those carbohydrates are not used up.

3) This increases the amount of energy the athlete has stored in their muscles, giving them plenty of energy for the event.

Timing Protein Intake Helps Muscle Growth

1) The body isn't as good at storing protein as it is at storing some other nutrients. This means power athletes, like weightlifters and body-builders, will eat protein regularly so it's available for muscle growth and repair.

2) They might also take in protein at certain times to maximise their muscle growth. E.g. within an hour of doing a workout — when the muscles need to recover and repair themselves, so need protein to rebuild.

3) Also, your body repairs itself while you sleep, so power athletes will make sure they get plenty of protein before bed.

Warning: cheese before bed may cause nightmares...

I preferred the sequel — 'Carbo-reloaded: revenge of the spuds'...

That's the end of the diet pages. Make sure you know who benefits from carbohydrate loading and timing protein intake, and why. Once you've got it, do this Exam Practice Question and make yourself a celebratory sandwich...

Q1 Justify whether a weightlifter or a triathlete would benefit more from carbohydrate loading. [3 marks]

Somatotypes

Somatotype means the basic shape of your body. Your somatotype can affect your suitability for a particular sport. You only need to read this page if you're doing the AQA course.

Somatotypes are Body Types

There are three basic somatotypes — ectomorph, mesomorph and endomorph.
Very few people are a perfect example of one of these body types — pretty much everyone is a mixture.
You can think of these basic somatotypes as extremes — at the corners of a triangular graph.

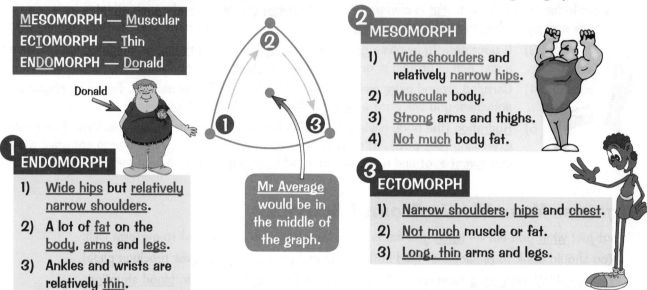

MESOMORPH — Muscular
ECTOMORPH — Thin
ENDOMORPH — Donald

Donald

① ENDOMORPH

1) Wide hips but relatively narrow shoulders.
2) A lot of fat on the body, arms and legs.
3) Ankles and wrists are relatively thin.

Mr Average would be in the middle of the graph.

② MESOMORPH

1) Wide shoulders and relatively narrow hips.
2) Muscular body.
3) Strong arms and thighs.
4) Not much body fat.

③ ECTOMORPH

1) Narrow shoulders, hips and chest.
2) Not much muscle or fat.
3) Long, thin arms and legs.

Different Somatotypes suit Different Sports

Certain body types are better suited for certain sports — the right body type can give you an advantage.

Endomorphs are usually best at activities like wrestling and shot-put — where weight and a low centre of mass (see p25) can be an advantage.

E.g. in sumo wrestling, being heavy and having a low centre of mass makes it much harder for your opponent to throw you around the wrestling ring.

Ectomorphs suit activities like the high jump and long-distance running — where being light and having long legs is an advantage. They don't usually suit activities where strength is important.

E.g. high jumpers need to be light so they have less weight to lift over the bar. The taller the jumper, the shorter the distance they (and their centre of mass) have to travel to be able to get over the bar.

Mesomorphs are suited to most types of activity:

1) They're able to build up muscle relatively quickly and easily — which gives them an advantage in any activity where strength is important. E.g. sprinting, tennis, weightlifting...

2) Mesomorphs also have broad shoulders, which make it easier for them to be able to support weight using their upper body. This can be a huge advantage in activities like weightlifting and gymnastics.

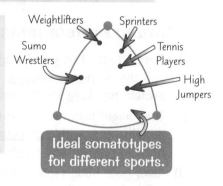

Weightlifters   Sprinters
Sumo   Tennis
Wrestlers   Players
                 High
                 Jumpers

Ideal somatotypes for different sports.

What do you call a shape-shifting ghost? An ectomorph...

Remember — nearly everybody's a mixture of these basic body types. Learn the names well — it'd be a bad mistake to get the three somatotypes confused. Now, check you've got it with this Exam Practice Question...

Q1   State **one** example of a sport that an ectomorph is well suited to do. Justify your answer.   [2 marks]

Optimum Weight

If you're doing the OCR course, skip this page. If you're doing Eduqas, you only need the energy balance bit.

Optimum Weight Depends on Different Things...

Your optimum weight is roughly what you should weigh for good health, based on these four factors that differ from person to person:

1) HEIGHT — The taller someone is, the larger their body, so the higher their optimum weight.

2) BONE STRUCTURE — some people have a larger or more dense bone structure than others. This means their skeleton will be heavier, so their optimum weight will be higher.

3) MUSCLE GIRTH — this is a measurement of the circumference of (the distance around) your muscles when they're flexed. Some people naturally have more muscle than others — they'll have a larger muscle girth and a higher optimum weight.

4) GENDER — men and women naturally have different body compositions. Men usually have larger bone structures and more muscle than women, so men generally have higher optimum weights.

Your Body Mass Index (BMI) score is calculated using your height and weight. A BMI of under 18.5 means underweight, over 25 means overweight and over 30 means obese. BMI doesn't take into account muscle girth or bone structure, so it can incorrectly classify healthy, muscular people as overweight or obese. See page 73 for an example of some BMI data.

Optimum Weight will Vary for Different Sports...

A sportsperson's optimum weight is the weight at which they perform best. Optimum weight will vary depending on the activity or sport — e.g. a sumo wrestler will want to be heavier than a mountain climber.

1) Some sports require competitors to be within a certain weight class — e.g. a boxer's optimum fighting weight needs to be within their weight division.

2) In sports like rugby or American football, players have a large amount of muscle mass because they need strength and power. This means their optimum weight will be higher.

3) Similarly, some sports require performers to be light — e.g. a gymnast needs to hold their own body weight, so being light is an advantage.

4) Endurance athletes will want to be lighter than sprinters as they have to carry their weight for longer. Sprinters need large amounts of muscle to generate power, so have a higher optimum weight.

Your Energy Balance controls your Weight

How much energy you need from food depends on how much you use up through bodily processes (like breathing and digestion), daily activities and exercise. This is also affected by your age, height and gender. Your energy balance is the relationship between the energy you take in and the energy you use:

1) If you take in more energy than you use, you have a positive energy balance. Spare energy is stored as fat, which causes you to gain weight.

2) If you don't take in enough food to match the energy you need, you have a negative energy balance. Your body makes up the difference by using up the energy stored in body fat. This causes you to lose weight.

3) If you want to maintain a healthy weight, you need to make sure you balance your energy intake with the energy you use up. This is called a neutral energy balance.

4) Energy from food is measured in calories (Kcal). On average, an adult male needs 2500 calories a day, and an adult female needs 2000 calories a day.

Energy In   Energy Out

How many star jumps 'til I can have the cake?

There's a ton of things on this page you need to know. You could say this page is heavy with facts. It's certainly not lightweight. So, make sure you learn it all and tip those scales in your favour for the exam...

Q1   Give **two** reasons why two women of the same height could have different optimum weights.   [2 marks]

Revision Questions for Section Four

That's it for Section Four. Give yourself a little time to digest all that information (ho ho ho), then fingers on buzzers for the Section Four revision questions...

* Try these questions and tick off each one when you get it right.
* When you've done all the questions for a topic and are completely happy with it, tick off the topic.
* The answers can all be found by looking back over pages 45 to 53.

Health, Fitness and Well-being (p45-46) ☑

1) Give two physical health benefits of physical activity.
2) What effect does regular aerobic exercise have on blood pressure?
3) Which bone disease can weight-bearing exercise help prevent?
4) How can exercise make you feel good?
5) Give two social health benefits of sport.
6) Physical activity can increase your confidence. Is this a physical, emotional or social benefit?

Lifestyle Choices and a Sedentary Lifestyle (p47-48) ☑

7) How can diet have a positive effect on health?
8) What effect does alcohol have on blood pressure?
9) State two health problems that can be caused by smoking.
10) Give one long-term effect of not getting enough sleep.
11) Define a 'sedentary lifestyle'. How is it connected to obesity?
12) What are two health risks associated with a sedentary lifestyle?

Diet and Nutrition (p49-51) ☑

13) What is a 'balanced diet'?
14) Are proteins macronutrients or micronutrients? How about vitamins?
15) Name a macronutrient that provides lots of energy that can easily be used by the body.
16) How does protein help you recover after exercise?
17) Give two reasons why the body needs vitamins.
18) Which mineral is necessary for making red blood cells?
19) Explain what happens to your blood when you become dehydrated.
20) State two effects of overhydration.
21) What role does fibre play in a balanced diet?
22) What type of athlete uses carbohydrate loading?
23) Why might a sprinter have a diet high in protein?

Somatotypes and Optimum Weight (p52-53) ☑

24) Name the three somatotypes and write down their main characteristics.
25) For each somatotype, write down one sport it is suited to.
26) Give three factors that affect optimum weight.
27) What weight classification is someone with a BMI score of 26? Why might this be misleading?
28) If you take in more energy from food than you use up, do you lose weight?
29) How can an athlete maintain a healthy weight?

Learning Skills

Learning skills and performing them well is really important in PE. If you're doing the AQA or Edexcel course, don't worry about knowing all the characteristics of a skilful movement — they won't come up in your exam.

A Skill is Something You Learn

A 'motor skill' is just a skill that involves movement.

1) Skill is a word we use all the time. Here's what it means in PE:

> A SKILL is a learned ability to bring about the result you want with confidence and minimum effort.

2) So a skill is something you've got to learn. You can't be born with a skill, although you might learn it more easily than other people. How easily you learn a skill is based on your ability:

> ABILITY is a person's set of characteristics that control their potential to learn a skill.

Different Characteristics make a Movement Skilful

There are some characteristics that make a movement or performance skilful:

PRE-DETERMINED — With any skilled movement, you always have a pre-determined result in mind — you know what you want to do before you start. E.g. if you're passing the ball to someone in hockey you know what type of pass you're going to use and who you want to pass it to.

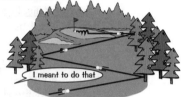
I meant to do that

EFFICIENT — A skilled movement should be efficient and use the minimum amount of energy/time. E.g. a good swimming technique can help you swim faster and for longer.

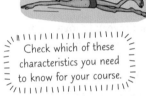

Check which of these characteristics you need to know for your course.

COORDINATED — Skilled movements are coordinated — they use two or more parts of the body together to get the maximum effect. E.g. a vault in gymnastics requires good arm and leg coordination to produce the necessary lift.

FLUENT AND CONFIDENT — A skilled athlete is able to flow confidently from one skilled movement to another, e.g. punch combinations in boxing.

Man I'm gorgeous...

AESTHETIC — Skilled movements are controlled and look good. In some sports, like gymnastics and figure skating, your skill is judged by the appearance of your movements. Skilled players make skilled movements and techniques look easy, while less skilled players and performers can look awkward and uncoordinated.

EFFECTIVE AND ACCURATE — A skilled athlete can perform a skill accurately to get the result they want.

TECHNICAL — A skilled movement uses the correct technique.

CONSISTENT — Skilled athletes can reliably perform a skill in different conditions.

GOOD DECISION MAKING — Skilled athletes can make good decisions to adapt to their environment, e.g. making tactical decisions to exploit an opponent's weaknesses.

You can describe Skill Level with the Stages of Learning

Beginners and experienced performers of a skill (and people in between) are at different 'stages of learning':

You only need to know this for the Eduqas course.

THE COGNITIVE STAGE	THE ASSOCIATIVE STAGE	THE AUTONOMOUS STAGE
They've just started learning the skill and are still a beginner.	They've learned the techniques involved in the skill, and are focusing on improving them.	They're experienced at performing the skill and can do it almost automatically.

Performers of different skill levels should be coached on their skills in different ways (see pages 58-59).

Quick — get learning while there's skill time...

Phew — who knew there was so much to know about being skilful in sport... Have a go at this Practice Question.

Q1 Explain the importance of efficient technique for the skill of marathon running. [2 marks]

Skills and Practice

This page is all about the different types of <u>skill</u>, and the different ways you should <u>practise</u> them. There are loads of definitions here, so check which ones you need for your course before you look at this page.

There are Different Types of Skill

1) There are different ways to <u>classify</u> skills:

OPEN VS CLOSED SKILLS

1) An <u>open skill</u> is performed in a <u>changing environment</u>, where a performer has to <u>react</u> and <u>adapt</u> to <u>external factors</u>. E.g. during a <u>football tackle</u>, you need to adapt to things such as the position of other players on the pitch.

2) A <u>closed skill</u> is always performed in the same <u>predictable environment</u> — it's <u>not</u> affected by external factors. E.g. when <u>breaking off</u> in snooker, the conditions are <u>the same</u> every time.

LOW VS HIGH ORGANISATION SKILLS

1) A <u>low organisation skill</u> is one which can easily be <u>broken down</u> into different parts that can be practised <u>separately</u>. E.g. the front crawl stroke in swimming.

2) A <u>high organisation skill</u> is one which <u>can't</u> easily be <u>broken down</u> into different parts that can be practised separately, because the parts of the skill are <u>closely linked</u>. E.g. a cartwheel.

BASIC VS COMPLEX SKILLS

1) A <u>basic skill</u> (or 'simple' skill) is one which <u>doesn't</u> need much <u>concentration</u> to do, e.g. running.

2) A <u>complex skill</u> is one which needs <u>lots of concentration</u> to do, e.g. a volley in football.

SELF- VS EXTERNALLY-PACED SKILLS

1) A <u>self-paced skill</u> starts when a performer <u>decides</u> to start it. Its <u>pace</u> is controlled by the <u>performer</u>.

2) An <u>externally-paced skill</u> starts because of <u>external factors</u> which also control the <u>pace</u> of the skill. E.g. an <u>opponent's actions</u> in <u>football</u> might determine <u>when</u> and <u>how quickly</u> you need to <u>pass</u> the ball.

GROSS VS FINE SKILLS

1) A <u>gross skill</u> involves <u>powerful</u> movements performed by <u>large muscle groups</u>, e.g. the long jump.

2) A <u>fine skill</u> uses <u>smaller</u> muscle groups to carry out <u>precise</u> movements that require <u>accuracy</u> and <u>coordination</u>, e.g. throwing a dart.

2) Most skills come somewhere <u>in between</u> these classifications. You can show this by putting skills on a '<u>continuum</u>' (or '<u>scale</u>') with one category on each end.

3) For example, you can compare the "openness" of skills by putting them on a <u>scale</u> like this one:

4) You can also put sport skills on a scale using the other skill classifications, e.g. a scale from basic to complex skills.

CLOSED   OPEN

You need Practice to Improve a Skill

⌇⎜⎜⎜⎜⎜⎜⎜⎜⎜⎜⎜⎜⎜⎜⎜⎜⎜⎜⎜⎜⎜⎜⎜⎜⎜⌇
The breaks can also be used to get <u>feedback</u> on a skill (see p58-59).
⌇⎜⎜⎜⎜⎜⎜⎜⎜⎜⎜⎜⎜⎜⎜⎜⎜⎜⎜⎜⎜⎜⎜⎜⌇

There are <u>six</u> different types of practice you need to know about:

<u>MASSED</u> — This means practising the skill continuously <u>without a break</u>. It works well to improve <u>basic skills</u>.

<u>DISTRIBUTED</u> — This means practising with <u>breaks</u> for <u>rest</u> or <u>mental rehearsal</u> (see p60). It works well to improve <u>complex skills</u> — you might need a <u>break</u> because the skill is <u>difficult</u>.

<u>FIXED</u> — This means repeating the same technique in <u>one situation</u> over and over again. This makes it useful for practising <u>closed skills</u>. It is sometimes known as doing '<u>drills</u>'.

<u>VARIABLE</u> — This means repeating the technique in <u>different situations</u> that you might need to use it in. It's useful for practising <u>open skills</u>.

<u>WHOLE</u> — This means practising the whole technique in <u>one go</u>. It's good for practising <u>basic skills</u> — they're easier to learn all in one go.

<u>PART</u> — This means <u>breaking</u> a skill down into <u>parts</u> and practising each bit <u>separately</u>. It's good for improving <u>complex skills</u> that might be difficult to learn all in one go.

Bobsleighers say 'packed ice' makes perfect...

Think about how these practice types would be suited to learners at different skill levels. Try a Practice Question...

Q1 Justify the positioning of 'catching a cricket ball' on the open-closed continuum on this page. [3 marks]

Goal Setting

Setting goals and targets can often seem a bit of a hassle. But if you put the effort in and set them properly, not only do you have something to aim for, but reaching your targets can make you feel ace.

Goal Setting can Help you Train

1) Goal setting means setting targets that you want to reach so you can improve your performance.

2) Goal setting helps training by giving you something to aim for, which motivates you to work hard. Also, reaching a goal can boost your confidence and help your emotional well-being (see p46).

3) You can set yourself a performance goal, an outcome goal, or a combination of both:

> PERFORMANCE GOALS — these are based on improving your own personal performance.
> OUTCOME GOALS — these are focused on performing better than other people, e.g. winning.

4) Most of the time, it's better to set performance goals — especially if you're a beginner. Winning might be an unrealistic goal if you're new to a sport, and it can be demotivating if you lose.

5) Also, you can't usually control the result of an outcome goal, as it will depend on how well other people perform.

Goal Setting Should be SMART

When you're setting targets make sure they're SMART.

There are a few different versions of what 'SMART' stands for here — check which one you need for your course.

S ➡ SPECIFIC: Say exactly what you want to achieve.
1) You need to have a specific target and outline exactly what you need to do to achieve it.
2) This makes sure you're focused on your goal.
3) E.g. 'My goal is to swim 1000 m continuously'.

M ➡ MEASURABLE: Goals need to be measurable.
1) This is so you can see how much you've progressed towards your goal over time — so you stay motivated to train.
2) E.g. 'My goal is to run 100 m in under 12 seconds'.

'A' can also stand for 'accepted' or 'agreed' — you should agree your goals with your coach.

A ➡ ACHIEVABLE: You need to make sure your targets are set at the right level of difficulty. If a target's too easy, it won't motivate you. If it's too difficult, you might start to feel negative about your performance, and give up.

R ➡ REALISTIC: Set targets you can realistically reach.
1) This means making sure you have everything you need to be able to fulfil your target.
2) That could mean being physically able to do something, or having enough resources (time, money, facilities...) to be able to reach your target.
3) This is so you stay determined during training — if it's not realistic, you could be put off.

'R' can also stand for 'recorded' — you should keep track of your progress.

T ➡ TIME-BOUND/TIME-PHASED/TIMED: Set a deadline for reaching your goal.
1) You need a time limit to make sure your target is measurable.
2) Meeting short-term target deadlines keeps you on course to reach your long-term goals in time.
3) This keeps you motivated — you'll want to train to achieve your goal in time for your deadline.

> As well as setting targets, you need to make sure you review them regularly. This is so you can see how much you've progressed towards your goal and what else you need to do to achieve it.

Goal setting — jumpers for goal posts...

Make sure you know what SMART stands for and how it can improve performance. Now try a Practice Question...

Q1 An athlete sets herself a goal to increase her running speed in six weeks.
State **one** principle of SMART goal setting that this goal does not apply. Explain your answer. [2 marks]

Guidance and Feedback

To learn or improve a skill, you might need some guidance and feedback to help you.

Guidance — How to Perform or Develop a Skill

There are lots of different types of guidance a coach or trainer can give:

Have a look at p56 for definitions of the different skill types.

1) <u>VERBAL</u> — An explanation in <u>words</u> of how to perform a technique.

ADVANTAGES
1) Can be <u>combined</u> with other types of guidance.
2) Helpful for <u>experienced performers</u> who'll understand any technical language.
3) Can give guidance <u>during</u> a performance. This is especially useful for improving <u>open skills</u>.

DISADVANTAGES
1) Less useful for teaching <u>high organisation</u> and <u>complex skills</u> which are difficult to explain.
2) Could be <u>confusing</u> for a beginner if it uses <u>complicated language</u>.

2) <u>VISUAL</u> — <u>Visual clues</u> to help you perform a technique. A coach could use <u>demonstrations</u> or <u>videos</u> and <u>diagrams</u> of a technique to show how it should be performed.

ADVANTAGES
1) Works well for <u>beginners</u> — they can <u>copy</u> the skill.
2) Can be used to teach <u>low organisation</u> skills — each part of the skill can be shown step by step.

DISADVANTAGES
Less useful for teaching <u>complex</u> and <u>high organisation</u> skills — they're more complicated and <u>difficult to copy</u>.

3) <u>MANUAL</u> — When the coach <u>physically moves</u> your body <u>through</u> the <u>technique</u>. For example, a coach might guide your arms when you're practising a golf swing.

Learning by doing an action is known as kinaesthetic learning.

ADVANTAGES
1) You can get the "<u>feel</u>" of a skill before doing it on your own.
2) Works well to teach people of <u>all skill levels</u>.

DISADVANTAGES
1) A performer could start to <u>rely</u> on it and not be able to perform a skill <u>without</u> it.
2) Difficult to use with <u>big groups</u> of learners.

4) <u>MECHANICAL</u> — Guidance given using <u>sport equipment</u>, e.g. a harness in trampolining.

ADVANTAGES
1) Useful for teaching <u>beginners</u> — they can feel <u>safe</u> while practising a new skill that might normally be <u>dangerous</u>, e.g. a somersault.
2) Helpful for teaching <u>complex</u> and <u>high organisation</u> skills.

DISADVANTAGES
1) A learner might be <u>unable</u> to perform the skill without the help of the <u>equipment</u>.
2) Difficult to use in <u>large groups</u>.

Feedback — Finding Out How You Did

1) Feedback can be either <u>intrinsic</u> or <u>extrinsic</u>:

<u>INTRINSIC</u> — <u>you</u> know how well you did the technique because of what it '<u>felt</u>' like. This works best for <u>experienced</u> performers — they can judge whether or not they've performed well.

<u>EXTRINSIC</u> — <u>someone else</u> tells you or shows you what happened, and how to <u>improve</u>. This is suited to <u>beginners</u> — they don't have the experience or knowledge to accurately assess their own performance.

2) These types of feedback can be either <u>concurrent</u> or <u>terminal</u>:

<u>CONCURRENT FEEDBACK</u> is received <u>during</u> a performance.
<u>TERMINAL FEEDBACK</u> is received <u>after</u> a performance.

3) You can use feedback to work out your <u>strengths</u> and <u>weaknesses</u> and come up with an <u>action plan</u> to improve your performance.

Verbal guidance is just what it sounds like...

Make sure you know the advantages and disadvantages of these guidance types. You need to be able to decide whether a certain type is suitable for teaching a particular group a skill. Here's an Exam Practice Question to try...

Q1 Evaluate the use of verbal and manual guidance to improve a beginner's performance in golf. [9 marks]

Using Feedback

More about <u>feedback</u> on this page, and how it's <u>applied</u> when you <u>perform</u> or <u>practise</u> a skill.
If you're doing the Edexcel course, you can skip this page and go straight on to the next one.

Feedback can Focus on Different Aspects of a Skill

1) The <u>information</u> in feedback can focus on <u>different parts</u> of a skill or movement. It might focus on:

- <u>KNOWLEDGE OF PERFORMANCE</u> — did you use the correct <u>movements/technique</u>? This can be <u>extrinsic</u> or <u>intrinsic</u>. This type of feedback works well for <u>experienced</u> performers — it helps them to '<u>fine-tune</u>' a skill that they can already perform.
- <u>KNOWLEDGE OF RESULTS</u> — what was the <u>outcome</u>? This is usually <u>extrinsic</u> and can include <u>data</u>, e.g. your time in a race. This is useful for <u>inexperienced</u> performers — they need to be told whether or not they achieved the <u>right result</u>.

2) Feedback could also focus on what you <u>did well</u> (<u>positive feedback</u>), or what you <u>didn't do well</u> and could <u>improve</u> (<u>negative feedback</u>).

3) It's better to <u>avoid</u> too much <u>negative</u> feedback with <u>beginners</u> — it can put them off learning the skill. <u>Positive feedback</u> is better — it helps them <u>remember</u> which parts of the movement they should repeat.

For an example of <u>interpreting feedback data</u>, see p74.

4) <u>Negative feedback</u> can be useful for <u>experienced performers</u>. It can help to <u>motivate</u> them by setting a goal for them to aim for.

Feedback is part of the Information Processing Model

The <u>information processing model</u> divides the <u>process</u> of performing or practising <u>skills</u> into <u>four stages</u>:

You don't need this bit for the <u>OCR</u> course.

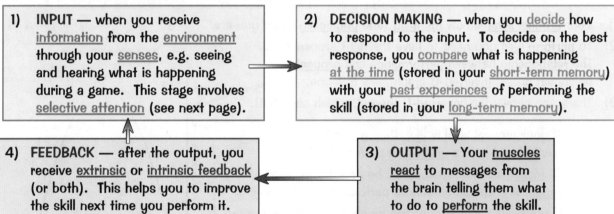

1) **INPUT** — when you receive <u>information</u> from the <u>environment</u> through your <u>senses</u>, e.g. seeing and hearing what is happening during a game. This stage involves <u>selective attention</u> (see next page).

2) **DECISION MAKING** — when you <u>decide</u> how to respond to the input. To decide on the best response, you <u>compare</u> what is happening <u>at the time</u> (stored in your <u>short-term memory</u>) with your <u>past experiences</u> of performing the skill (stored in your <u>long-term memory</u>).

4) **FEEDBACK** — after the output, you receive <u>extrinsic</u> or <u>intrinsic feedback</u> (or both). This helps you to improve the skill next time you perform it.

3) **OUTPUT** — Your <u>muscles react</u> to messages from the brain telling them what to do to <u>perform</u> the skill.

You can <u>apply</u> this model to <u>analyse</u> a sports skill. For example, when <u>taking a penalty</u> in football:

1) INPUT — You'd need to <u>pay attention</u> to the position of the goalkeeper in front of the net and <u>ignore</u> distractions like noise from the crowd.

2) DECISION MAKING — You'd decide on the <u>best way</u> to perform the penalty by using what you've done in your <u>previous practice</u> of penalties.

3) OUTPUT — Your brain would send information to your <u>muscles</u> to tell them <u>where</u> to aim the shot and how <u>powerfully</u> to kick the ball.

4) FEEDBACK — You'd receive <u>extrinsic feedback</u>, e.g. whether or not you <u>scored</u> the penalty, or your <u>coach</u> telling you what you did <u>right</u> or <u>wrong</u>. You might also get <u>intrinsic feedback</u>. You could <u>learn</u> from this feedback how you could perform a penalty <u>better</u> next time.

I'd make a PE joke — but it would only get negative feedback...

Make sure you learn which types of feedback work best for different skill levels. Here's a Practice Question to try.

Q1 A snowboarding instructor praises a beginner's stance on the snowboard.
Justify the use of this feedback in helping the beginner learn to snowboard. [3 marks]

Section Five — Sport Psychology

Mental Preparation

Who'd have thought it — <u>performing well</u> in sport is about <u>the mind</u> as well as the body...
If you're doing the Edexcel or Eduqas course, you only need to look at the first half of this page.

You can Mentally Prepare for Sport

1) Being <u>mentally prepared</u> is all about being able to get in the 'zone'.

2) It can help you stay <u>focused</u>, <u>confident</u> and <u>motivated</u>, keep control of your emotions and <u>cope with stress</u> so you can perform at your best.

Now remember Lenny, stay focused on the game.

3) There are lots of different techniques to help you <u>mentally prepare</u>:

> 1) <u>MENTAL REHEARSAL</u> is <u>imagining</u> the <u>feeling</u> in the <u>muscles</u> when <u>perfectly</u> performing a skill.
>
> 2) <u>VISUALISATION</u> involves <u>imagining</u> what an aspect of your performance should <u>look like</u>. It can be used as part of <u>mental rehearsal</u>.
>
> 3) <u>DEEP BREATHING</u> can help <u>lower</u> your <u>heart rate</u> (which <u>increases</u> when you're <u>anxious</u>) and make you feel more <u>calm</u>.
>
> 4) <u>IMAGERY</u> is used when you <u>imagine</u> being somewhere or doing something that <u>relaxes</u> you.
>
> 5) <u>POSITIVE SELF-TALK/THINKING</u> is telling yourself <u>positive things</u> that will <u>motivate</u> you or <u>reassure</u> you that you can <u>perform well</u>.
>
> 6) <u>SELECTIVE ATTENTION</u> is focusing on important things that will help you perform well, and <u>ignoring</u> things that <u>aren't important</u>.

Techniques 1-5 are also called 'stress-management techniques' — they help lower your <u>arousal level</u> (see below).

4) Practising your skills during a <u>warm-up</u> can also help you mentally prepare (see page 40).

Your Arousal Level shouldn't be Too High or Too Low

1) Your <u>arousal level</u> is how <u>mentally</u> (and <u>physically</u>) <u>alert</u> you are.

2) To <u>perform well</u> you need to have the right arousal level. The <u>relationship</u> between <u>performance</u> and <u>arousal</u> can be shown on an '<u>inverted-U graph</u>', like this one:

3) The graph shows the '<u>inverted-U theory</u>', which says that:

> • If your arousal level is <u>low</u>, then you're not very excited and you're <u>unlikely</u> to perform well.
>
> • At <u>higher</u> arousal levels, you'll be <u>determined</u> and <u>ready</u>, and should be able to perform your skills <u>well</u>.
>
> • If your arousal level <u>rises too much</u>, you become <u>anxious</u> and <u>nervous</u>. You might become <u>tense</u>, which can cause you to '<u>choke</u>', so your performance will <u>suffer</u>. You might also become <u>overaggressive</u>.

If you're doing the <u>OCR course</u>, don't worry about this graph — you just need to know the effects of high or low arousal.

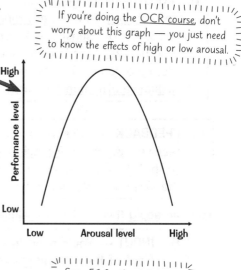

See p56 for the definitions of gross and fine skills.

4) The <u>ideal</u> arousal level <u>varies</u> for different skills in sport.

5) <u>Gross skills</u> require <u>higher arousal</u> levels. E.g. when tackling in <u>football</u>, a <u>higher arousal</u> level will help you commit to putting all of your <u>effort</u> into getting the ball. But if your arousal level is <u>too high</u>, you might end up <u>hurting</u> another player when you tackle them.

6) When performing a <u>fine skill</u>, you need a <u>lower arousal</u> level. E.g. when <u>fielding</u> in cricket, a <u>lower arousal</u> level will help you keep your hands <u>steady</u> to catch the ball. But your arousal level shouldn't be <u>too low</u> — or you won't be <u>alert enough</u> to move into a good position to catch the ball.

Mentally rehearse your exam for guaranteed success...

Being mentally prepared can really help your performance — so it's lucky that there are some handy techniques to help you on your way to being mentally ready for sport. Learn all about them, then try this Practice Question.

Q1 Suggest **one** reason why a football player might use mental rehearsal before taking a penalty. [1 mark]

Emotion and Personality

This is the last page in this section now — it'll cover types of <u>motivation</u>, <u>aggression</u> and <u>personality</u>.
If you're doing the Edexcel or OCR course, you can skip straight on to the revision questions on the next page.

Motivation makes you Want to Do Well

1) <u>Motivation</u>'s about how <u>keen</u> you are to do something.
   It's what <u>drives you on</u> when things get difficult — your <u>desire</u> to succeed.

2) Motivation can be either <u>intrinsic</u> (from yourself) or <u>extrinsic</u> (from outside).

Official CGP tug o' war champion

INTRINSIC MOTIVATION	EXTRINSIC MOTIVATION
Motivation from the <u>enjoyment</u> and good <u>feelings</u> you get from taking part in physical activity and sport, e.g. pride, high self-esteem.	Motivation through <u>rewards</u> from other people/ sources. This can be <u>tangible</u> (you can <u>touch it</u>, e.g. trophies, money) or <u>intangible</u> (you <u>can't touch it</u>, e.g. applause, praise from a coach).

3) <u>Intrinsic motivation</u> is usually seen as the <u>most effective</u> — you're more likely to <u>try hard</u> in sport and <u>carry on</u> playing it in the long run if you <u>enjoy it</u>.

4) <u>Extrinsic motivation</u> can also be really <u>effective</u>. Rewards or praise about your performance can make you feel <u>good</u> about yourself — so you're more likely to <u>want</u> to perform well again.

5) But if you <u>don't like</u> a sport, <u>extrinsic</u> rewards on their own probably <u>won't motivate</u> you to <u>try</u> very hard at it, or play it <u>regularly</u>. They work better when you're already <u>intrinsically</u> motivated.

6) But some people think that too many <u>extrinsic</u> rewards can actually <u>reduce</u> your <u>intrinsic</u> motivation — so you might start to <u>rely</u> on extrinsic rewards to feel <u>motivated</u>.

Aggression can be Direct or Indirect

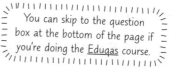
You can skip to the question box at the bottom of the page if you're doing the <u>Eduqas</u> course.

<u>Aggression</u> doesn't have to be <u>violent</u> — when it's used <u>properly</u>, it can improve your <u>performance</u> in sport.

1) <u>Direct aggression</u> involves <u>physical contact</u> with another person, e.g. pushing against the opposing team in a <u>rugby scrum</u> so you can win the ball.

2) <u>Indirect aggression</u> doesn't involve physical contact — a player gains an advantage by aiming the aggression at an <u>object</u> instead. E.g. a golfer performing a drive would use indirect aggression towards the golf ball to hit it powerfully to the green.

Introverts and Extroverts like Different Sports

The <u>type of sport</u> you like can be affected by your <u>personality</u>. You can describe someone as an <u>introvert</u> or an <u>extrovert</u> based on what their personality is like — most people are somewhere <u>in between</u>.

<u>INTROVERTS</u> are <u>shy</u>, <u>quiet</u> and <u>thoughtful</u> — they like being <u>alone</u>.	<u>EXTROVERTS</u> are more <u>sociable</u> — they're <u>talkative</u> and prefer being with <u>other people</u>.
1) Introverts usually prefer sports that they can do <u>on their own</u>.	1) Extroverts might get <u>bored</u> when they're alone, so they usually prefer <u>team sports</u>.
2) They tend to like sports where they'll need <u>fine skills</u>, <u>high concentration</u> and <u>low arousal</u>.	2) They also tend to like <u>fast-paced</u> sports that need <u>gross skills</u> and <u>low concentration</u>.
3) For example, <u>archery</u>, <u>snooker</u> and <u>athletics</u> are all suited to introverts.	3) For example, <u>hockey</u>, <u>rugby</u> and <u>football</u> are well-suited to extroverts.

Chocolate biscuits — an effective form of extrinsic motivation...

There's a handy way to remember what 'intrinsic' and 'extrinsic' mean. 'Intrinsic' starts with 'in', so it comes from inside you. 'Extrinsic' starts with 'ex', just like 'exit', so it comes from outside. Here's a Practice Question.

Q1 Which one of the following is an example of tangible extrinsic motivation?
   A Praise from a teammate   **B** Wanting to succeed   **C** A medal   **D** Enjoying a sport   [1 mark]

Revision Questions for Section Five

Section Five has come to an end, so let's see how much you've learned.

- Try these questions and tick off each one when you get it right.
- When you've done all the questions for a topic and are completely happy with it, tick off the topic.
- The answers can all be found by looking back over pages 55 to 61.

Skills and Practice (p55-56) ☐

1) Explain what is meant when a movement is described as 'pre-determined'. ☑
2) What is the difference between an open and a closed skill? ☑
3) Which type of skill can be broken down into separate parts? ☑
4) Which type of skill needs lots of concentration to perform? ☑
5) Which type of skill has its pace controlled by the person performing it? ☑
6) Give two examples of an open skill. ☑
7) What is the difference between massed and distributed practice? ☑
8) Explain the difference between fixed and variable practice. ☑

Goal Setting (p57) ☑

9) Why might a performer set themselves a goal? ☑
10) What is the difference between performance and outcome goals? Why are performance goals better? ☑
11) What do the letters in SMART stand for? ☑
12) Explain the meaning and benefits of each element of SMART. ☑
13) Why should you review your targets and goals regularly? ☑

Guidance and Feedback (p58-59) ☐

14) What is guidance? ☑
15) What is verbal guidance and why is it more suited to more experienced performers? ☑
16) What is visual guidance? Why is it effective for teaching low organisation skills? Why is it less effective for teaching high organisation skills? ☑
17) Give an example of manual guidance. ☑
18) What is mechanical guidance? ☑
19) What disadvantage do manual and mechanical guidance have in common? ☑
20) What is feedback? ☑
21) Explain the difference between intrinsic and extrinsic feedback. ☑
22) Explain what is meant by:
    a) Concurrent feedback
    b) Terminal feedback ☑
23) What is the difference between knowledge of performance and knowledge of results? ☑
24) Describe the four stages of the information processing model. ☑

Mental Preparation, Emotion and Personality (p60-61) ☑

25) How might an athlete mentally prepare for a performance? ☑
26) Explain the 'inverted-U theory'. ☑
27) Explain why intrinsic motivation is usually more effective than extrinsic motivation. ☑
28) Explain the difference between direct and indirect aggression. ☑
29) What type of sport do introverts usually enjoy? Give an example. ☑

Influences on Participation

Participation rates are how many people take part in sport or other physical activities. Whether you participate in sports, and the type of sports you play, can be affected by lots of different factors...

People Influence the Activities you do

Your family and friends can have a big influence on whether you do sport, and which sports you choose.

FAMILY

1) Parents might encourage their children to take up sports, or discourage them.

2) If your parents or siblings play sport, or are interested in it, you're familiar with sport from a young age. You may also have more opportunities to take part.

FRIENDS

1) You're influenced by the attitudes of people your own age (your peers), especially your close friends...

2) For example, if all your mates play football, you're likely to play football with them. If your mates say that sport is rubbish and don't play it, you might do less sport.

ROLE MODELS

People who excel in their sport can become role models for their sport and inspire people to be like them. This encourages more people to participate in their sport.

The media can help create role models — see p67.

Your Gender may Influence whether you do an Activity

Although things are getting better, there's still a real gender divide in participation. Surveys carried out by Sport England show that, overall, fewer women participate regularly in sport than men.

1) This may be because many women's events have a lower profile than men's, as they get less media coverage. This has meant that in many sports there are fewer female role models to inspire younger generations to take up the sport.

2) Less media coverage also means there is less sponsorship available for women's sport, meaning there are fewer opportunities and less money for women to do sport at a high level.

3) Gender tagging — outdated and stupid attitudes about some things being "women's activities" and others being "men's activities" — might also affect what sports you decide to take up.

4) This includes ridiculous gender stereotypes about it 'not being feminine' to get sweaty or muddy, or to play sports where you need aggression. Similarly, stereotypes about masculinity may also mean boys are expected to play more aggressive sports or mocked for enjoying activities seen as less 'manly'.

Ethnicity and Religion can have an Effect too

1) Sometimes your religious beliefs or ethnic background can influence the physical activity you do.

> E.g. many Muslim women keep their bodies covered up. This may mean they're less likely to participate in activities such as swimming because of the clothing that's expected to be worn.

2) Religious festivals and days may impact on when you can play sport. For example, some Christians won't play sport on a Sunday because it's the Sabbath, so could not join a Sunday league team.

3) Racism and racial abuse used to be a huge problem in sport. Campaigns against racism, such as the Let's Kick Racism Out Of Football campaign, have helped to raise awareness of the problem. Also, punishments for players and fans who are racist are now much more severe than they used to be.

4) Governing bodies have also tried to help create more positive role models to inspire and engage younger generations to participate.

5) Policies like the 'Rooney Rule' in American football, which says that teams must interview at least one ethnic minority candidate for any head coaching job, are also helping to create more opportunities.

That was such a good somersault — you're my roll model...

Just because these things can affect your participation in a sport doesn't mean that they should. Everyone should be able to participate in whatever sport they would like to without worrying about their ethnicity or their gender...

Q1 Explain **one** way in which your friends could affect whether or not you participate in sport. [2 marks]

Influences on Participation

Another page of <u>influences on participation</u> — so many influences, so little time... <u>Disability</u> can influence what activities you do, and so can your <u>job</u>, where you <u>live</u> and how much <u>money</u> you have...

Disability can Influence how Active you are

1) Having a <u>disability</u> can limit the physical activities you can do. Studies show that participation rates for disabled people are lower than they are for non-disabled people.

2) The <u>opportunities</u> in sport and <u>access to sporting facilities</u> for disabled people used to be few and far between.

3) Nowadays, there are many <u>schemes</u> set up to give disabled people <u>more opportunities</u> to exercise and take part in activities within their physical limits. These schemes focus on:

- <u>Adapting</u> sports so that they're more accessible for disabled people — e.g. wheelchair basketball or handcycling.

- <u>Creating new sports</u> specifically for disabled people — like boccia (a game like bowls that can be played from a wheelchair) and goalball (a game like handball that blind people can play).

- <u>Including</u> disabled people in activities alongside non-disabled people. This helps to <u>challenge stereotypes</u> about disabled people as well as giving disabled people the <u>opportunity</u> to enjoy a <u>wide range</u> of activities.

4) Disabled sporting events are now given a lot more <u>media coverage</u> than they once were. The Paralympics now gets extensive <u>media coverage</u>, like the Olympics.

5) This media coverage is helping to <u>change people's attitudes</u> towards disability and sport.

6) It's also helping create many more <u>disabled role models</u> (like <u>Dame Tanni Grey-Thompson</u> and <u>Ellie Simmonds</u>), which encourages more disabled people to get active.

Your Socio-Economic Group can also have an Effect

<u>Socio-economic groups</u> are just a <u>fancy</u> way of grouping people based on how much <u>money</u> they have, where they <u>live</u> and the type of <u>job</u> they do.

Yaaaar, I'm a Yuppie — a Young, Upwardly-mobile Pirate.

- "Working class", "middle class" and "young professional" are all examples of socio-economic groups.

Recent studies seem to show that, in general, people in <u>lower socio-economic groups</u> are <u>less likely</u> to regularly take part in sport. The <u>kinds</u> of activities people do can also be affected by their socio-economic group.

1) Most sports cost <u>money</u>. This means that some people can't <u>afford</u> to take part.

2) Lots of sports — like <u>horse riding</u>, <u>skiing</u>, <u>sailing</u> and even <u>cycling</u> — require specialist <u>equipment</u> and <u>clothing</u>. This can be very <u>expensive</u>, so could prevent people from taking part.

3) Some sports require special <u>facilities</u> — like <u>ski slopes</u> or <u>ice rinks</u>. If you don't live in an <u>area</u> with these sorts of facilities, you won't easily be able to <u>do</u> those sports.

4) If you don't have access to a <u>car</u> or good <u>public transport</u> to get to the facilities, this makes it a lot harder to participate. You'll be more likely to do a <u>more accessible</u> sport like football or basketball.

5) If you work <u>shifts</u> or <u>irregular hours</u> it can be hard to join clubs or groups that meet in the evenings or at the weekend.

6) Playing sport can also require a lot of <u>free time</u>. If you <u>work long hours</u>, or have <u>family commitments</u> like caring for children, you might just <u>not</u> have the <u>time</u>.

We're all under the influence...

You need to understand how all these personal factors can have an effect on participation rates and what sports people participate in. And now, treat yourself and have a pop at this Exam Practice Question...

Q1 Suggest **one** reason why having a disability might affect your participation in physical activity. [1 mark]

Influences on Participation

That's right, it's another page of influences on participation. Just like the rest of them, there's a bunch of facts to get your head around. So, buckle up, get comfortable and set your brain to 'memorise'...

Age can Limit the Activities you can do

1) Some sports are more popular than others with different age groups.

2) Most people aged 16-30 have loads of choice for physical activity.

3) People over 50 are more physically limited in the sports they can choose. They tend to do less strenuous activities like walking or swimming.

4) Some sports, such as weightlifting or endurance events, can potentially damage a young person's body. Competitions in these sorts of activities often have a minimum age restriction.

5) Young people often have more spare time to do sport. As people get older and have careers and families, there's less time available for playing sport.

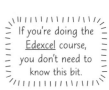

> If you're doing the Edexcel course, you don't need to know this bit.

PE in Schools can have a big effect on Participation

PE in schools plays a big role in shaping people's feelings towards sport and exercise:

1) PE classes and after-school activities are a way for students to try out lots of different sports. This allows students to become familiar with lots of activities, which might encourage regular participation. It's really important that schools offer a wide range of activities, so there's something for everyone. This will encourage more students to join in and enjoy sport:

- Some students are put off by PE at school because they find it awkward or embarrassing.
- Allowing students to choose what activities they would like to do, and listening to students' suggestions about improving PE, can make students more willing to take part.
- Some students do not enjoy the competitive nature of sport, so offering non-competitive activities in PE is a good idea — e.g. fitness classes or yoga.
- Schools can also bring in outside agencies to help with coaching and sports development.

2) Having a really good PE teacher, or sport's coach at a club, can really help to inspire people too. The flip side of this is that a bad experience in PE could end up putting you off sports and exercise.

3) The facilities a school has available can limit what activities it can offer. Also, grimy old changing rooms and equipment can mean some students just aren't inspired to join in with PE at all.

4) In PE you should learn physical literacy. This means you have basic skills like running, jumping, throwing, catching and swimming that you can use as a starting point for learning lots of new activities and sports. These skills allow you to go on and take part in physical activity throughout your life.

Even the Environment has an effect

> This was a terrible idea...

> This bit is just for the OCR course.

1) If you live nowhere near mountains and snow, the opportunities to compete in many winter sports will be few and far between.*

2) In very hot and very cold climates, it might not be possible to be outside and active for long periods of time, which can affect participation in sports.

3) Pollution levels can force people to remain indoors, which makes it harder to participate in a lot of sports.

4) The layout of a city can dramatically affect participation in running, cycling and other outdoor activities — without pavements, cycle lanes and green spaces like parks, there is nowhere to do these things.

5) Really mountainous regions may struggle to have flat areas for creating pitches, so participation in many team sports can be difficult.

*No one told the Jamaican bobsleigh team this.

I keep dropping my books — I think I'm physically illiterate...

All these influences work together to shape our attitude towards physical activity — make sure to get 'em learned...

Q1 Give **two** ways that schools can encourage students to enjoy sport and physical activity. [2 marks]

Influences on Participation

You need to know about ways of <u>improving</u> participation rates, and how to <u>interpret data</u> about participation.

Learn these Three Strategies for Encouraging Participation

There are three main ways of improving participation rates: <u>promotion</u>, <u>provision</u> and <u>access</u>:

PROMOTION

1) Participation can be <u>promoted</u> through <u>advertising campaigns</u> — like Sport England's This Girl Can campaign launched in 2015, which <u>challenges stereotypes</u> about women in sport.

2) Big <u>sporting events</u>, like the London Olympics in 2012, help to create <u>role models</u> and <u>promote active lifestyles</u>. <u>Media coverage</u> of events like the Paralympics and the Women's World Cup in football can also help <u>inspire</u> higher participation rates and <u>challenge stereotypes</u>.

3) More locally, <u>clubs</u> and <u>facilities</u> can be promoted to local residents through <u>local advertising</u>, so they know what's <u>available</u> in their area.

PROVISION

1) Providing <u>facilities</u> and well-trained <u>staff</u> can help to encourage more people to take up sports and activities.

2) It's important that these facilities cater to a <u>wide range</u> of people by offering plenty of <u>variety</u> — including offering a range of activities for disabled and elderly folk.

3) <u>Leisure centres</u> provide a wide range of classes and activities, and have trained staff and coaches to help all kinds of people be <u>active</u> and <u>healthy</u>.

4) <u>PE classes</u> and <u>clubs</u> after <u>school</u> help provide students with opportunities to participate in sport and exercise (see p65).

ACCESS

1) Having <u>access</u> to facilities can be a problem, especially in <u>rural</u> areas. Also, sometimes it can be difficult for families without a <u>car</u> to get involved in lots of sporting activities.

2) The government can help by providing good <u>public transport</u> links. Organisations like Sport England help clubs buy <u>minibuses</u> and other methods of <u>transportation</u>. Some <u>disabled</u> people may also require <u>specialist equipment</u>, like ramps, to be able to use these methods of transport.

3) Access can be improved by clubs and facilities being <u>reasonably priced</u>, so people can <u>afford</u> to use them.

You'll Need to Interpret Data about Participation Rates

In the exam, you'll need to be able to <u>analyse graphs</u> showing participation rates for different sports and activities.

1) You may get asked to <u>compare activities</u>, e.g. to say which activity has <u>increased</u> or <u>decreased</u> most from one point to another.

2) The <u>bigger</u> the <u>difference</u> between these <u>two points</u>, the <u>bigger</u> the <u>increase</u> or <u>decrease</u>.

3) For example, the graph on the right shows that:

- Participation in <u>running</u> <u>increased</u> more than football or cycling from <u>07/08</u> to <u>10/11</u>.

- Participation in <u>football decreased</u> more than cycling or running from <u>11/12</u> to <u>12/13</u>.

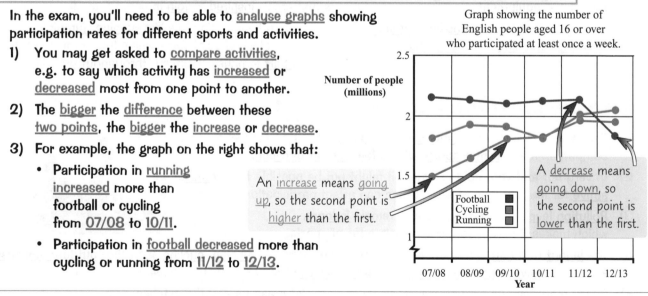

Graph showing the number of English people aged 16 or over who participated at least once a week.

An <u>increase</u> means <u>going up</u>, so the second point is <u>higher</u> than the first.

A <u>decrease</u> means <u>going down</u>, so the second point is <u>lower</u> than the first.

Football
Cycling
Running

Participation — you've got to be in it to win it...

You could get a graph showing participation rates for different groups — e.g. rates for men and women. You might need to use the reasons covered on these pages to explain the differences too. Now, Practice Question time.

Q1 Using the graph above, which of these sports had the highest participation rate in 2012-13?

   A Football   **B** Cycling   **C** Running   **D** Golf   [1 mark]

Commercialisation of Sport

Lots of people are raking in cash from sport these days. This is called commercialisation. Here are the facts...

Commercialisation Means Making Money

1) The commercialisation of sport is all about making money from it.

2) A lot of money comes from sponsorship — if people are going to see it, companies will slap their name on it, whether it's a person, team, league, stand, trophy, mascot or ball. This is great advertising for the sponsor. As well as money, sponsors might also provide equipment, clothing or facilities.

3) Money also comes from the media — organisations involved in mass communication — like television companies, radio broadcasters and newspapers.

4) The media pay so they can cover the sport, which means people will buy their newspaper or watch their TV show. Some companies sell sport on TV, or over the Internet, as a subscription package too.

5) Broadcasting sports on television and the Internet means it now reaches an even larger, global audience — this is known as the globalisation of sport. This all makes sponsorship even more valuable.

6) Social media gives fans new ways to interact with their favourite sports stars and teams. This keeps sponsors of those teams and players in the public eye, which promotes them even more.

7) Sports also make money through selling tickets to events, and merchandise.

Sport, the Media and Commercialisation are all Connected

Sport, the media and sponsorship have grown to depend on one another — this is called the 'golden triangle'. There are advantages and disadvantages to this relationship for the sponsor, the sport, the players, the spectators and the officials.

SPONSORSHIP AND SPORT

1) Sponsorship deals mean companies can associate their name with the prestige of successful sportspeople and teams. This is an effective form of advertising, which helps the sponsor to make more money.

2) These deals mean big money for sport — which can be spent on development, e.g. of a new stadium or facilities. This benefits the players and the spectators. This money can also pay for technology to help officials (see p69).

3) Sponsorship money also means players and officials can be paid good wages, and players can train full-time. This benefits everyone, because they will perform better.

SPONSORSHIP AND THE MEDIA

1) The more media coverage a sport gets, the more people watch it. This makes sponsorship more valuable, as it can reach a larger audience.

2) This increases the likelihood of sponsorship and means the sport and players can demand more money for their sponsorship deals.

THE MEDIA AND SPORT

1) The media pay for the rights to cover sporting events, which provides investment for sports to develop at lower levels.

2) Media coverage makes more people aware of the sport, so more people may play it or watch it.

3) Media coverage of elite players and athletes can create role models who inspire people to play.

4) This can make players into superstars. But, the downside is that players are hounded by the media and their private lives are all over the news.

5) Also, the media can hold so much power over sport that they'll change things:
   - The number of games played, or the timings of matches, might be changed so more matches can be shown. This risks injury to players through lack of rest, and might mean spectators miss a game because it's not at a convenient time.
   - Also, rules may be changed — e.g. the tiebreaker set was brought into tennis to make matches shorter.

6) Being able to watch on TV or the Internet, rather than going to the game, can save fans money. However, fewer fans buying tickets means losses in ticket sales for the sport and a poorer atmosphere at the stadium for spectators.

7) The media's analysis of refereeing decisions puts sports officials under a lot of pressure.

8) Media analysis of games can also educate spectators, so they understand the sport better.

I don't write these jokes for the money — I do it for the love, man...

Get this commercialisation stuff memorised and the marks will flow like famous footballers' sponsorship deals.

Q1 Explain **two** ways that media interest in a sport can encourage more people to take part. [4 marks]

Commercialisation of Sport

Sponsorship can be a little complicated. You need to know that it has its downsides and that not all types of sponsor are suitable. Read on to find out about the dark side...

Sponsorship Isn't All Great

Why's he playing?

His Dad sponsors the team.

1) Sometimes, the money is only available for the top players and teams, so benefits the elite — not the sport as a whole.

2) It could all turn nasty — if an athlete gets injured, loses their form or gets a bad reputation they could lose their sponsorship deal. Bad behaviour by an athlete reflects badly on the sponsor too and could damage the company's reputation.

3) Sometimes athletes have to fulfil contracts with their sponsor — they might have to turn up at a special event or appear in a TV advert (even if they don't want to).

4) Athletes can get into trouble with their sponsor if they're spotted using another company's products.

5) If a team really needs a sponsor's money, this puts the sponsor in a position of power. This means they can influence the team's playing style or team selection.

6) In some sports where there are breaks in play, adverts will be shown. The game won't be allowed to restart until the advert break is finished, which can be quite boring for spectators in the stadium.

Some Sponsors are Inappropriate

Sponsorship brings in loads of money, but you have to be careful not to promote the wrong image, especially in youth sports:

1) Cigarette and tobacco companies aren't allowed to sponsor sports in the EU. This is because their products are harmful and unhealthy.

2) Alcoholic drinks companies are allowed to sponsor some sports, but this can be bad as it gives alcohol a false image of health. The same is true for unhealthy food companies.

3) Also, as sport is watched by children, advertising alcohol and fast food could be encouraging young people to drink or eat unhealthily.

You'll Need to Interpret Data About Commercialisation

It's another one of those fun data bits. In your exam you could be asked to interpret data about the commercialisation of sport.

1) For example, the graph on the right shows the total amount spent each year on shirt sponsorship (that's companies paying to have their logo on the front of a team's shirt) in the Premier League.

2) The graph shows that every year since 2010, spending on shirt sponsorship in the Premier League has increased.

3) So there's an upward trend in spending on shirt sponsorship — and if the graph carried on past 2015, you'd expect it to keep on going upwards.

4) You can also see that the biggest increases in spending were from 2011 to 2012 and from 2014 to 2015 — shown by the line going up more steeply.

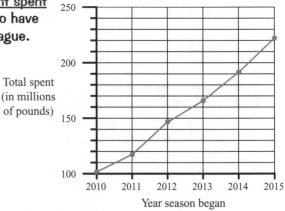

A graph showing the amount spent on shirt sponsorship in the Premier League between 2010 and 2015.

Total spent (in millions of pounds)

Year season began

CGP CGP CGP CGP (CGP — Official Sponsors of page 68)...

It's important that you can weigh up the pros and cons of sponsorship, especially when it comes to fast-food and alcohol companies. Have a go at this Exam Practice Question to check you've got it...

Q1 Assess the positive and negative impact on an under-12's football team of being sponsored by a fast-food company.

[6 marks]

Technology in Sport

There's loads of technology used in sport and you need to know all about it for the AQA and Eduqas courses.

Technology can help Players to Perform Better

1) Lots of the technology used today is designed to help athletes perform better at their sports. This benefits spectators as well as performers, as new levels of sporting excellence are achieved.

2) New materials are used to make sports equipment and clothes more effective — from shoes to swimming costumes to tennis rackets. This helps players reach new levels of performance.

3) Improvements to training facilities, like all-weather pitches, mean that training doesn't have to stop for bad weather. This means more time can be spent training, so performances will improve.

4) There have also been developments to make sports safer, like better protective clothing and better playing surfaces. Also, medical technology can help athletes recover from injuries quickly and safely.

Tony used ICT to improve his dropkick technique.

5) Video footage and 3D modelling software can be used by coaches to analyse an athlete's movement. This can be done to a very high degree of accuracy, so an athlete's technique can be fine-tuned. In events like the 100 m sprint, where winning may come down to a few milliseconds, this level of accuracy is really important.

6) All this technology is expensive though. This can mean that only people with lots of money can compete at the highest level.

7) There is a worry that technology can give athletes an unfair advantage over their competitors. If sport becomes less about the abilities of the athletes and more about the technology they're using, it kind of stops being interesting for spectators.

Technology can help Officials to make Correct Decisions

Many sports now make use of technology during matches to help referees and umpires.

Out!

Hawk-Eye (tennis) — Hawk-Eye uses a set of six cameras to track and predict the path of the ball. It's used so that players can challenge the decision of whether shots are in or out.

Decision Review System (DRS) (cricket) — players are allowed to challenge an umpire's decision and have it reviewed by the third umpire, who uses various bits of technology (including Hawk-Eye) to decide whether the on-field umpire was correct or not.

Television Match Official (TMO) (rugby union) — the TMO is an extra official who watches video replays. The referee on the pitch can consult with the TMO to help them make key decisions.

Goal-line technology (football) — there are cameras pointed at each goal that are used to tell whether or not the ball has crossed the goal line.

ADVANTAGES

1) All these systems help to make the sport more fair, which benefits spectators and players by avoiding the frustration of wrong decisions.

2) They help officials to make valid and reliable decisions, even in marginal situations. This lessens the pressure on them.

3) The DRS in cricket has shown that the umpires are right most of the time. This has led to increased respect for umpires.

4) Sponsors can use the breaks in play that some of these technologies cause to show adverts.

DISADVANTAGES

1) These systems are expensive to install, so are only used at the top end of sporting leagues.

2) The fact that things can be reviewed could undermine the authority of the officials on the pitch. This could lead to players contesting every decision the referee makes.

3) Referring to a video replay can sometimes take a long time. Some people worry that these breaks disrupt the flow of play and can also be boring for spectators.

'Owzaaaat?!

I could be a TMO — they just sit around watching sport on TV...

Cyborg-boxing and techno-jocks — bring on the technology in sport I say. I, for one, welcome our new robot overlords... What rhymes with 'Sham Cactus Session'? That's right, Exam Practice Question. Now, hop to it...

Q1 Discuss the positive and negative impact that technology can have on sport. [9 marks]

Sporting Behaviour

This page is about good and bad <u>behaviour</u> in sport. Turns out taking your ball home if you're <u>losing</u> isn't okay.

Sportsmanship is About Being Fair and Humble

Being a good sportsperson is <u>more</u> than just playing by the rules. You also have to show good '<u>sportsmanship</u>' (even if you lose) and <u>uphold</u> the '<u>contract to compete</u>'.

<u>Sportsmanship</u> means being <u>honest</u>, <u>sticking to the rules</u> and treating your opponents with <u>respect</u>.

The <u>contract to compete</u> is an <u>unwritten</u> <u>agreement</u> between competitors to respect the '<u>spirit of the game</u>'.

You only need to know this for the <u>AQA</u> course.

1) This means no <u>rubbing it in</u> the opposition's face if you <u>win</u>. And no going <u>off in a huff</u> if you <u>lose</u>.
2) It also means observing the <u>etiquette</u> of an activity — following <u>unwritten rules</u> and <u>conventions</u>. E.g.:
   - In cricket, a batsman might choose to '<u>walk</u>' if they think they've been caught <u>out</u> — even if the umpire has <u>ruled</u> them <u>not out</u>.
   - In football, players will kick the ball <u>out of play</u> if a member of the other team goes down <u>injured</u>.

Gamesmanship and Deviance — Types of Poor Behaviour

<u>Gamesmanship</u> is gaining an advantage by using tactics that <u>seem unfair</u>, but <u>aren't</u> against the rules.

<u>Gamesmanship</u> is <u>not</u> actually cheating — but it can come <u>quite close</u>. A lot of the techniques are about <u>breaking</u> up the <u>flow</u> of a game, or <u>distracting</u> your opponents:

1) <u>Time-wasting</u> in football is when players deliberately <u>faff about</u>. This <u>runs down</u> the <u>clock</u> and <u>breaks up</u> the <u>flow</u> of the game.
2) In tennis, some players make loud <u>grunting</u> or <u>shrieking</u> noises when they <u>hit the ball</u> to try and <u>intimidate</u> or <u>distract</u> their opponent.
3) In basketball, a manager might call a <u>timeout</u> just as the opposition win a <u>free throw</u>. This is to try and make them <u>overthink</u> the shot.

<u>Gamesmanship</u> does <u>not</u> normally result in <u>punishment</u> for the players, although if it is taken <u>too far</u> referees might get <u>involved</u>.

<u>Deviance</u> is behaviour that goes against the <u>moral values</u> or <u>laws</u> of the sport.

<u>Deviance</u> is <u>breaking the rules</u>. Sometimes it involves <u>cheating</u> to gain an <u>advantage</u> in the game:

1) Using <u>performance-enhancing drugs</u> or <u>blood doping</u> (see p43) are both deviance because they give you an <u>unfair</u> advantage.
2) '<u>Professional fouls</u>', like tripping someone to get ahead of them, are also deviance.

Other times it's being <u>violent</u> and <u>aggressive</u>:

3) Cuban taekwondo athlete Angel Matos was <u>banned</u> from the sport for life after deliberately <u>kicking a referee</u>.
4) Boxer Mike Tyson and footballer Luis Suarez have both been in trouble for <u>biting</u> their opposition.

<u>Violence</u> in sport can happen because players are <u>frustrated</u> with the result, or with decisions made by the referee. It can also come from players being overly <u>emotional</u> or <u>competitive</u>.

<u>Deviance</u> is <u>punished</u> by sports officials to <u>discourage</u> players from doing it:

1) For really <u>serious offences</u>, like using performance-enhancing drugs or biting, players may be <u>banned</u> from competing. There could also be a <u>hefty fine</u>.
2) For deviance like <u>fouling</u> an opponent, the referee or umpire may punish players by <u>removing</u> them from the field of play <u>temporarily</u> — the '<u>sin bin</u>', or <u>permanently</u> — a <u>red card</u> or <u>disqualification</u>.

See p76 for an example of <u>data</u> about ethical issues in sport...

Most forms of deviance happen <u>more</u> at the <u>higher levels</u> of a sport because there is so much <u>at stake</u> — e.g. the money and the fame brought about through the commercialisation of sport (see p67).

Footballers ought to be gracious in defeat — they use 'em enough...

I know, it's easy to get confused between sportsmanship and gamesmanship. Just remember that sportsmanship is about 'being a good sport'. Now, I've got an Exam Practice Question fresh from the oven and still warm for you.

Q1   Describe the difference between deviance and gamesmanship.   [2 marks]

Spectator Behaviour

Big sporting events draw big crowds. This has both advantages and disadvantages. You only need this page if you're doing the AQA course.

> *You only sing when you're winning, sing when you're wiiiiinnniiiing....*

Spectators create an Atmosphere

1) Crowds at sporting events create an atmosphere and this adds to the excitement, making the event more enjoyable for spectators and players.

2) Also, this can create a 'home-field advantage' — the 'home' team perform better because they're in familiar surroundings with more fans supporting them. This can also intimidate the opposition.

3) However, sometimes all those spectators can put pressure on the performers, who end up performing worse because they are nervous and afraid to make mistakes.

4) Having spectators at sporting events for younger people (like youth leagues in football) can put more pressure on the kids who are taking part. This can discourage children from taking up activities, so can negatively affect participation rates (see pages 63-66).

5) At big events, it takes a lot of planning and money to make sure spectators are safe. With large groups there's the chance of crowd trouble and hooliganism...

> *Pah, hooligans the lot of you...*

Hooliganism is when fans Become Aggressive

Hooliganism is rowdy, aggressive and sometimes violent behaviour of fans and spectators of sport. You need to know what causes hooliganism and how it can be prevented...

CAUSES

1) Rivalries between fans. These rivalries might be built up by the press and the media so they seem even more important. This hype can cause fans to take the match too seriously.

2) Some fans might have been drinking, or even taking drugs, which can fuel aggression and violence.

3) Frustration with decisions made by officials, or just frustration with how the match is going, can lead to spectators getting angry.

4) Some people see hooliganism as a display of masculinity, or a way of fans proving themselves to be macho. Peer pressure can make people feel they have to join in. There could also be a 'gang mentality', where people feel less responsible for their actions because they're in a group.

METHODS OF PREVENTION

1) Kick-offs can be made earlier for games where it's likely there will be trouble. This leaves less time between the pubs opening and the start of the game, so fans will be less drunk during the game. Alcohol restrictions can also be brought in to control buying alcohol within the stadium.
   - However, fans often get round this by drinking more before they go to the game. Also, having earlier kick-offs can make it inconvenient for travelling fans to get to the game.

2) Making every stadium 'all-seated' so fans don't have to stand. This is safer because people are less packed together. It's also easier for stewards and police to get to troublemakers.

3) Fans can be segregated (sat in separate sections) to stop fighting inside the ground. Sometimes home and away fans enter and leave the ground at different times.
   - This doesn't help prevent violence outside of the stadium though, and it can mean it takes longer for fans to get into or out of the stadium, which is annoying for the fans.

4) The number of police and stewards at games can be increased, which boosts security in the ground. Also, video surveillance and other technology can be used to monitor crowds.
   - It can be very expensive to install all this technology and pay extra police and stewards.

5) For fans who have committed hooliganism in the past, there are banning orders and travel restrictions, e.g. confiscating passports. This means that the worst offenders aren't at games.

6) There have been lots of campaigns to educate fans about the harm that's caused by hooliganism.

Hooliganism — a silly word but a serious issue...

For the methods of preventing hooliganism, it's important you learn their drawbacks. It's Practice Question time...

Q1 State **two** reasons why hooliganism might occur at a football match.   [2 marks]

Revision Questions for Section Six

That's <u>Section Six</u> done and dusted — now be a <u>good sport</u> and have a go at these <u>revision questions</u>.
Try these questions and <u>tick off each one</u> when you <u>get it right</u>.
- When you've done <u>all the questions</u> for a topic and are <u>completely happy</u> with it, tick off the topic.
- The answers can all be found by <u>looking back over pages 63 to 71</u>.

Influences on Participation (p63-66) ☑

1) Give one way that your family and friends might influence your participation in sport. ☑
2) How can your gender influence what sports you participate in? ☑
3) How can the media help improve participation rates amongst the disabled? ☑
4) What is meant by a socio-economic group? ☑
5) Outline one way that the amount of money you have could affect your participation in sport. ☑
6) Describe two ways that your age can limit your participation in physical activities. ☑
7) Give one example of a sporting activity that is inappropriate for a very young person to participate in. ☑
8) What's meant by 'physical literacy'? How can physical literacy impact on your participation in sport? ☑
9) Give two ways that the environment you live in can affect what sports you take part in. ☑
10) Explain how sports participation rates can be improved by promotion, provision and access. ☑
11) How do you spot an increase in a participation rate on a line graph? ☑

Commercialisation of Sport (p67-68) ☐

12) What does 'commercialisation' mean? ☑
13) Give one effect of increased media coverage on a sport. ☑
14) Give one advantage and one disadvantage of sponsorship for a sport. ☑
15) If a sports team gets media coverage, what might happen to the value of their sponsorship deals?
Give a possible reason for this happening. ☑
16) How can increased media coverage increase participation in a sport? ☑
17) Why do companies sponsor sports? ☑
18) Give one way an athlete could lose their sponsorship deal. ☑
19) Which of these cannot sponsor an EU football team: a) a car manufacturer, b) a tobacco company? ☑
20) Give an advantage and a disadvantage of a brewery sponsoring a youth games tournament. ☑

Technology in Sport (p69) ☑

21) Outline three ways technology can help an athlete perform better. ☑
22) Give an advantage and a disadvantage of using technology to help officials during a match. ☑

Sporting and Spectator Behaviour (p70-71) ☑

23) Give a definition and an example of:
a) Sportsmanship
b) Gamesmanship
c) Deviance ☑
24) Is time-wasting in football an example of gamesmanship or deviance?
What about a 'professional foul'? ☑
25) Name one possible punishment an athlete could face if they're caught blood-doping. ☑
26) Is deviance more likely or less likely to happen in the higher levels of sport? Why? ☑
27) Give a definition of hooliganism. Name one thing that can cause hooliganism. ☑

Using Data

You've got to be comfortable with interpreting data displayed in graphs and tables. Luckily for you, these five pages will go through how you do it. And you thought you could get away from maths by taking PE...

There Are Two Different Types of Data

You can collect two different types of data — qualitative data and quantitative data:

The easiest way to remember the difference is 'quantitative' sounds like 'quantity' — which means 'number of'...

> **Qualitative data describes something — it will be in words.**

> **Quantitative data measures something — it will be in numbers.**

1) Qualitative data can be collected through observation — e.g. 'the team played well', 'the athlete is strong' or 'the weather was cold'.

2) Or you can interview people. E.g. asking an athlete how they're feeling before a race might give you answers like "confident" or "well-prepared".

3) It's less easy to analyse than data in numbers.

1) Quantitative data measures things — e.g. 'time taken to finish a race' or 'weight of an athlete'.

2) All the fitness tests (see pages 27-31) give quantitative data, as the results are numbers. You can also use surveys or questionnaires to collect quantitative data.

3) Quantitative data can be represented in tables and graphs, and analysed easily.

You need to be able to Plot a Bar Chart from a Table

In the exam you might be asked to plot a bar chart using a table of data. You might know how to do this already, but it never hurts to go over it again. Below is a bar chart for the following data on BMI:

Number of students with each Body Mass Index (BMI) rating

BMI rating	Underweight	Healthy Weight	Overweight	Obese
No. of students	45	151	115	39

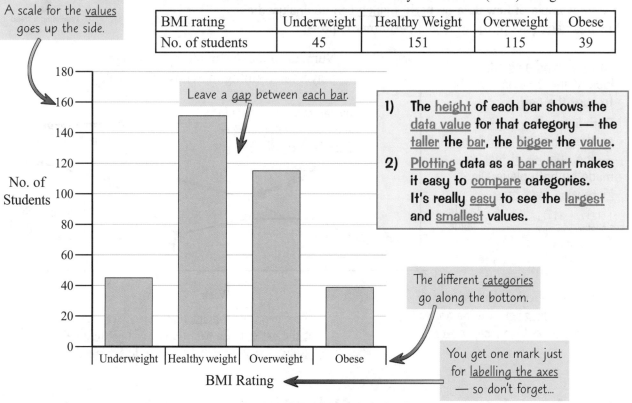

A scale for the values goes up the side.

Leave a gap between each bar.

1) The height of each bar shows the data value for that category — the taller the bar, the bigger the value.

2) Plotting data as a bar chart makes it easy to compare categories. It's really easy to see the largest and smallest values.

The different categories go along the bottom.

You get one mark just for labelling the axes — so don't forget...

Qualitatitative Qualatatave Quiltative — Oh, I give up...

Just from my experiences writing this page, I can promise you that it's frustratingly easy to mix up the words qualitative and quantitative, so double-check you're using the right one. Exam Practice Question time...

Q1 Outline **one** way that quantitative data can be used during training. [1 mark]

Using Data

This page is all about <u>line graphs</u> — you need to know how to <u>plot</u> them and how to <u>analyse</u> them.

You can Plot a Line Graph from a Table

In the exam, you might be asked to plot a <u>line graph</u> from a <u>table</u>. You might know how to do this already, but it <u>never hurts</u> to go over it <u>again</u>... I seem to be having déjà vu.

Riyad's results for the standing stork test

Week	1	2	3	4	5	6
Time (secs)	12	13.5	13	15.5	18	21

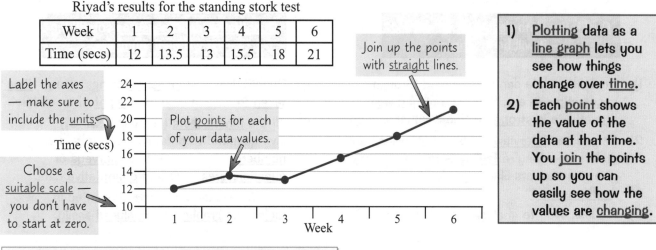

Label the axes — make sure to include the <u>units</u>.

Plot <u>points</u> for each of your data values.

Join up the points with <u>straight</u> lines.

Choose a <u>suitable scale</u> — you don't have to start at zero.

1) <u>Plotting</u> data as a <u>line graph</u> lets you see how things change over <u>time</u>.

2) Each <u>point</u> shows the value of the data at that time. You <u>join</u> the points up so you can easily see how the values are <u>changing</u>.

Analyse Graphs to spot Trends

To analyse a graph you can talk about <u>increases</u> and <u>decreases</u>, and <u>highest</u> and <u>lowest</u> values. This can also help you to spot <u>trends</u> and make <u>predictions</u>.

A <u>trend</u> is when a graph is generally <u>going up</u> or <u>down</u> over <u>time</u>.

Here's an example of how data on <u>performance</u> can be analysed as part of <u>feedback</u> (see p58), to help a performer improve.

Technicolour shorts are totally in right now...

Predicting a trend can be tough.

1) To <u>determine a trend</u>, look at the data <u>as a whole</u> to spot the <u>pattern</u>.

2) Both lines are <u>going up</u>, so they show <u>upward trends</u> — the <u>number of tackles</u> made by both players is <u>increasing over time</u>.

For another example of analysing data over time see p48.

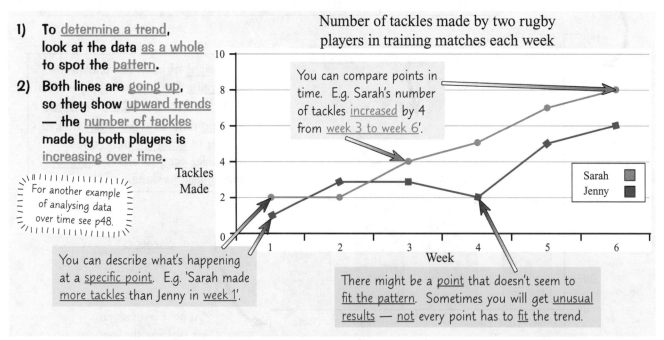

You can compare points in time. E.g. Sarah's number of tackles <u>increased</u> by 4 from <u>week 3 to week 6</u>.

You can describe what's happening at a <u>specific point</u>. E.g. 'Sarah made <u>more tackles</u> than Jenny in <u>week 1</u>'.

There might be a <u>point</u> that doesn't seem to <u>fit the pattern</u>. Sometimes you will get <u>unusual results</u> — <u>not</u> every point has to <u>fit</u> the trend.

Trends about data — amount of boredom is increasing over time...

All these graphs... I'm starting to lose the plot (ho ho ho). If you can analyse graphs and spot trends you'll breeze through any graph questions in the exam. Now, time to test those smarts with an Exam Practice Question...

Q1 Using the line graph about Sarah and Jenny above, identify which person had the bigger increase in tackles made from week 2 to week 6. [1 mark]

Using Data

Using data to help you evaluate and plan fitness training is dead important, so here's a whole page on it. You need to understand what the data is showing you as well as use your knowledge about physical fitness.

You can Analyse your Fitness over Time

1) You can measure the effect of your training by doing regular fitness tests, and comparing the data you get over time.

2) You need to be able to describe what the data shows, and say what this means about the training — i.e. if it's working or what changes are needed.

3) Here's an example of the kind of thing you might see in the exam:

Bryan is doing a training programme to improve his cardiovascular fitness and his muscular endurance...

Bryan's Fitness Test Results

Fitness Test	Weeks					
	1	2	3	4	5	6
Cooper 12-minute Run (distance in m)	1450	1490	1530	1600	1640	1690
One-Minute Sit-up test (no. of sit-ups)	45	46	45	46	44	45

The Cooper's Run data shows that Bryan is doing better at the Cooper 12-minute Run Test each week — he is running further in 12 minutes. So the training is improving Bryan's cardiovascular fitness.

The sit-ups data shows that the number of sit-ups Bryan can do is staying about the same, so the training is not improving his abdominal muscular endurance. This means Bryan may want to change his training programme to include more exercises that help improve his abdominal muscular endurance.

For more on fitness testing and training methods, see Section Three.

You can also look at national averages or ratings tables to understand how your scores in fitness tests compare with others in your age group or gender. For an example of this, see page 31.

Bar Charts can show Fitness Data

Remember that on a bar chart the heights of the bars show the data values. This means you can spot trends by looking at how the heights of the bars change over time.

Week 1 has the tallest bar, so Bryan's resting heart rate was highest in week 1.

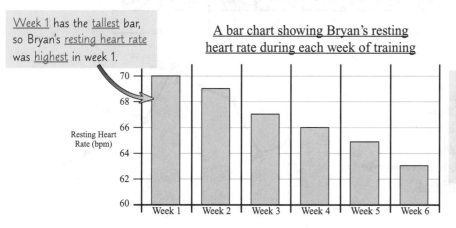

A bar chart showing Bryan's resting heart rate during each week of training

The trend here is that Bryan's resting heart rate is decreasing each week. This means that his cardiovascular fitness must be improving, as his heart is pumping blood more efficiently.

Top of the charts again — give it up for the 'tallest bars'...

It's really important you get good at using data about fitness to evaluate how effective an exercise programme is. Have another look over pages 27 to 30 to check you know all the fitness tests. Then do this Practice Question...

Q1 Using the bar chart above, what is Bryan's resting heart rate in week 4?

A 70 bpm   **B** 66 bpm   **C** 67 bpm   **D** 100 bpm   [1 mark]

Using Data

More data? Well okay, go on then — I know how much you love it. This page is about delicious pie charts and other less delicious uses of data. Needless to say, you have to learn it all, tasty or not so tasty...

You can Look at Data for Large Groups of People

You can also use data to understand what's going on for large groups of people.

1) Pie charts are a good way to compare different categories.

2) The amount of the whole chart a section takes up tells you the percentage in that category — the whole chart represents 100% (everybody).

3) These charts show that the netball club is almost entirely female, the football club is mostly male, and the badminton club is 50% male and 50% female.

For examples of using data to understand trends on a large scale, see pages 48, 66 and 68.

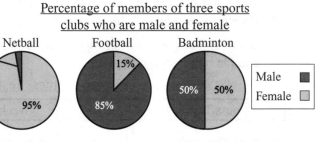

Percentage of members of three sports clubs who are male and female

Netball — 5%, 95%
Football — 15%, 85%
Badminton — 50%, 50%

Male / Female

Remember, percentages tell you the proportion of people in a category, not the actual number.

You can use Data to see the Effects of something

You might be asked to use data to assess the effectiveness of a decision.

EXAMPLE

1) Organisers of a regional Rugby Union tournament were becoming concerned at the high number of players being sin-binned during the competition. A player is sent to the 'sin-bin' for repeatedly breaking the rules or for a really bad foul.

2) From 2012, the organisers introduced a fine for the player being sin-binned to try and discourage players from foul play.

3) The table below shows the number of 'sin-bins' awarded at the tournament each year, from 2007 to 2015. You can analyse this data to see whether or not the fine has been effective:

The fine is introduced here.

Total number of sin-bins awarded each year

Year	2007	2008	2009	2010	2011	2012	2013	2014	2015
No. of 'sin-bins'	8	7	12	13	15	10	8	7	6

4) The fine will have been effective if it has led to fewer sin-bins.

5) As there has been a decrease in sin-bins awarded every year since the introduction of the fine, it looks like the fine has been effective.

6) Plotting a line graph of the data makes it easier to see the patterns.

The largest decrease in sin-bins comes between 2011 and 2012.

Number of sin-bins is increasing every year from 2008 to 2011.

Number of sin-bins (y-axis: 0 to 16)
Year (x-axis: 2007 to 2015)

Mmmmmm — pie charts....

When you're analysing a graph, try to think what could have caused any changes you see. Practice Question time...

Q1   Using the line graph above, state which year had the highest number of sin-bins awarded.   [1 mark]

Using Data

More ways to use <u>data</u> in <u>training</u>. <u>Heart rate data</u> is useful for working out how long you're exercising at <u>different intensities</u> for, and data collected about <u>performance</u> can help you check you're <u>achieving your goals</u>.

Heart Rate Data can be used to work out Exercise Intensities

By analysing data about someone's <u>heart rate</u> during exercise, you can work out <u>how long</u> they worked in each <u>target zone</u> for. Check back on page 34 for more information about <u>training target zones</u>. E.g.:

Joanna is <u>45 years old</u>, so her <u>maximum heart rate</u> is 220 – 45 = <u>175</u>.
This means the lower threshold of her <u>aerobic</u> target zone is <u>0.6</u> × 175 = 105 bpm,
and the lower threshold of her <u>anaerobic</u> target zone is <u>0.8</u> × 175 = 140 bpm.

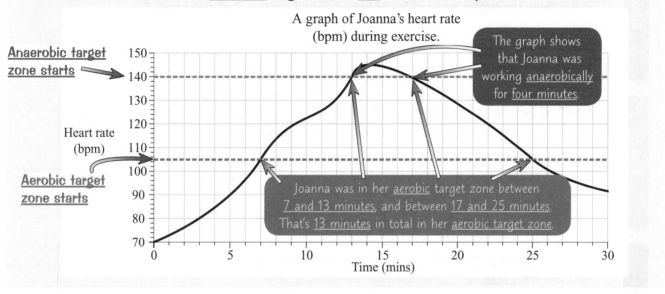

A graph of Joanna's heart rate (bpm) during exercise.

The graph shows that Joanna was working <u>anaerobically</u> for <u>four minutes</u>.

Anaerobic target zone starts

Heart rate (bpm)

Aerobic target zone starts

Joanna was in her <u>aerobic</u> target zone between <u>7 and 13 minutes</u>, and between <u>17 and 25 minutes</u>. That's <u>13 minutes</u> in total in her <u>aerobic target zone</u>.

Data can be used to help Monitor your Progress

Check back to page 57 to read about goal setting and SMART targets.

<u>Data</u> about your <u>performances</u> in <u>training</u> can help you to see whether or not you're <u>on track</u> to <u>meet your goals</u>. This is one of the reasons your <u>targets</u> need to be <u>measurable</u>. E.g.:

Nadège has just started cycling and she wants to <u>improve</u> her <u>average speed</u>.
She sets herself a goal to increase her average speed by <u>4 km/h</u> in <u>12 weeks</u>.

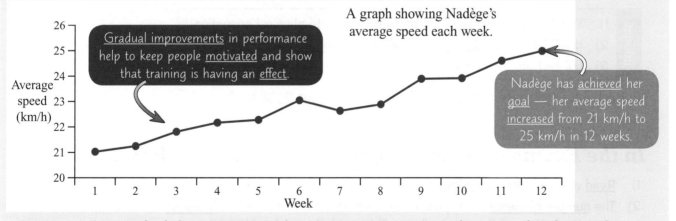

A graph showing Nadège's average speed each week.

<u>Gradual improvements</u> in performance help to keep people <u>motivated</u> and show that training is having an <u>effect</u>.

Nadège has <u>achieved</u> her <u>goal</u> — her average speed <u>increased</u> from 21 km/h to 25 km/h in 12 weeks.

Having a <u>goal</u> to aim for helps <u>motivate</u> people to <u>keep training</u>. In turn, this means that they are far more <u>likely</u> to <u>achieve</u> their goal — because they are <u>sticking</u> to their <u>training</u> regime. It's a <u>win-win</u> situation...

Goal setting — really important if you don't want runny targets...

That's it, you've made it to the end of the data section. In fact, you've made it to the end of the book. By now your head must be so jam-packed with knowledge that this last Exam Practice Question will be an absolute cakewalk...

Q1   Using the line graph above, did Nadège's average speed increase every week?   [1 mark]

Answering Exam Questions

Hurray — you made it to the end of the book. Now there's just the tiny matter (ahem) of the exams left to go. Here's what to expect in your exams and some exam tips to help you on your way to GCSE PE victory.

Here's what to Expect in the Exams

The way your exams are structured depends on the exam board you're with.

Edexcel
1) You'll sit two exams.
2) Paper 1 will test you on component 1 — 'Fitness and Body Systems'. It'll be worth 90 marks and will last 1 hour 45 minutes.
3) It'll include the topics covered in sections 1-3 and section 7 of this book.
4) Paper 2 will test you on component 2 — 'Health and Performance'. It'll be worth 70 marks and will last 1 hour 15 minutes.
5) It'll include the topics covered in sections 4-7 of this book.

AQA
1) You'll sit two exams. Each paper will be worth 78 marks and will last 1 hour 15 minutes.
2) Paper 1 will test you on 'The human body and movement in physical activity and sport'.
3) It'll include the topics covered in sections 1-3 and section 7 of this book.
4) Paper 2 will test you on 'Socio-cultural influences and well-being in physical activity and sport'.
5) It'll include the topics covered in sections 4-7 of this book.

For the AQA and OCR courses, the stuff on page 43 in section 3 will be tested in paper 2 — not paper 1.

OCR
1) You'll sit two exams. Each paper will be worth 60 marks and will last 1 hour.
2) Paper 1 will test you on component 1 — 'Physical factors affecting performance'.
3) It'll include the topics covered in sections 1-3 and section 7 of this book.
4) Paper 2 will test you on component 2 — 'Socio-cultural issues and sports psychology'.
5) It'll include the topics covered in sections 4-7 of this book.
6) Each paper will be split into two sections (section A and section B), and each section will be worth 30 marks.

Eduqas
1) You'll only sit one exam called 'Introduction to physical education'.
2) It will be worth 120 marks and will last 2 hours.
3) It'll test you on all the topics covered in sections 1-7 of this book.

In total, your exams (or exam) will make up 60% of your GCSE mark.

In the Exams — Read the Questions and Don't Panic

1) Read every question carefully.
2) The number of marks each question is worth is shown next to it in brackets, or at the bottom of the answer lines. This can be a good guide to the number of points you need to make and how long your answer should be.

The number of answer lines given in a question can also be a good guide to how much to write.

3) Make sure your answers are clear and easy to read. If the examiner can't read your handwriting, they won't be able to give you any marks.
4) Don't panic — if you get stuck on a question, just move on to the next one. You can come back to it if you have time at the end.

Answering Exam Questions

There are Three Types of Question you could be asked

Multiple-Choice — Cross the Right Box

1) The multiple-choice questions give you a choice of <u>four</u> or <u>five</u> possible answers to the question. All you need to do is choose <u>one option</u> that you think is the correct answer. They're worth <u>one mark</u> each.

2) It'll tell you on the exam paper <u>how</u> to answer the question — you'll either have to put a <u>cross</u> or <u>tick</u> in a box, or <u>shade</u> a circle next to the <u>correct answer</u>.

3) Make sure you only choose <u>one answer</u> — if you pick more than one you won't get the mark.

4) Don't worry if you make a <u>mistake</u> — there'll be instructions on how to <u>change</u> an answer if you need to.

5) If you <u>don't know</u> the answer to a question, <u>guess</u>. You don't lose marks for putting a wrong answer — if you guess, you've at least got a <u>chance</u> of getting it right.

Short-Answer Questions

1) <u>Short-answer</u> questions are usually worth between <u>one</u> and <u>five</u> marks.

2) Make sure you <u>read the question</u> carefully. If you're asked for two influences, make sure you give <u>two</u>, otherwise you won't get all the marks.

3) To get the marks, you'll need to <u>show</u> your <u>PE knowledge</u>, <u>apply</u> it to a situation, or use it to <u>analyse</u> or <u>evaluate</u> something. In questions worth more marks, you might need to do a <u>combination</u> of these.

Extended Writing Questions

1) <u>Extended writing</u> questions are worth between <u>six</u> and <u>ten marks</u>.

2) To answer these questions, as well as <u>showing</u> and <u>applying</u> your PE knowledge, you'll need to weigh up the <u>advantages</u> and <u>disadvantages</u> of something, or <u>analyse</u> how or why something happens.

3) At the end of your answer, you might need to write a <u>conclusion</u> where you make a <u>judgement</u>.

You get Marks for Meeting Different Assessment Objectives

1) <u>Assessment objectives</u> (<u>AOs</u>) are the things you need to do to <u>get marks</u> in the exams.

2) You'll be tested on <u>three</u> AOs:

> <u>Assessment objective 1</u> (AO1) is all about <u>demonstrating knowledge</u> and <u>understanding</u> of a topic.
> 1) Questions that test AO1 usually ask you to <u>state</u>, <u>define</u>, <u>describe</u> or <u>identify</u> something.
> 2) They could also get you to <u>label</u> a diagram or <u>complete</u> a table or sentence.

> <u>Assessment objective 2</u> (AO2) is about <u>applying knowledge</u> and <u>understanding</u> of a topic to a context.
> 1) Questions that assess AO2 might ask you to <u>explain why</u> or <u>how</u> something happens.
> 2) You'll sometimes need to <u>give examples</u> to back up your points.

> <u>Assessment objective 3</u> (AO3) is about <u>analysing</u> and <u>evaluating</u>.
> 1) Questions that test AO3 often start with words like <u>analyse</u>, <u>evaluate</u>, <u>assess</u>, <u>discuss</u> or <u>justify</u>.
> 2) <u>Analysing</u> just means breaking something down into <u>parts</u> or <u>stages</u> to explain it. This can include <u>analysing data</u> to explain what it <u>shows</u>.
> 3) To <u>evaluate</u>, <u>assess</u> or <u>discuss</u> something, you will need to weigh up its <u>advantages</u> and <u>disadvantages</u> in the context given in the question.
> 4) <u>Justifying</u> something means giving reasons <u>why</u> it's sensible.

3) A lot of questions will test <u>more than one</u> assessment objective — for example, if a question tells you to <u>evaluate</u> something (AO3), you'll also need to <u>demonstrate</u> your knowledge of the topic (AO1) and <u>apply it</u> to the situation in the question (AO2).

Answering Exam Questions

Don't Forget to Watch Your Spelling and Grammar

1) Some questions on the exam papers will test your written communication skills (otherwise known as 'how well you can write your answer'), as well as your amazing PE knowledge.

2) The questions where you get marks for your communication skills will be the longer ones that are worth at least 6 marks.

3) If you're doing the OCR course, any questions that assess the quality of your writing will have an asterisk (*) next to the question number (or letter) inside the paper.

4) You can pick up some easy marks just by making sure that you do these things:

> 1) Make sure you answer the question being asked — stay focused on the topic you're asked about, and don't waffle about anything that's not relevant.
>
> 2) Make sure your answer is organised. It's a really good idea to have a think about what you're going to cover in your answer, and jot it down in a quick plan before you start writing it. That way you can make sure you structure your answer well, and cover all the points you want to.
>
> 3) Write in full sentences and use correct spelling, grammar and punctuation.
>
> 4) Use the correct PE terminology.

Have a look at this Example Question and Answer

This example exam answer will show you how you might answer one of the extended answer questions.

15 Evaluate the use of continuous training and plyometric training to improve performance in cycling.

This applies knowledge of continuous training to the cyclist by saying what impact it will have on their performance.

This shows good knowledge of continuous training by talking about the components of fitness that it improves.

> Continuous training involves exercising aerobically for at least twenty minutes, and helps to improve both muscular endurance and cardiovascular fitness. Good muscular endurance would help to prevent muscle fatigue when cycling long distances, and a high level of cardiovascular fitness would allow a cyclist to continuously use their leg muscles over long periods on the bike. Continuous training can also be included as part of a normal cycling training session, allowing a cyclist to practise their overall technique.

This looks at the disadvantages of continuous training by talking about aspects of cycling performance that it doesn't improve.

This shows good application of knowledge by giving specific examples from cycling.

> However, the steady-state exercise involved in continuous training would not prepare a cyclist for the differing intensities involved in the sport, for example, when cycling on steep gradients, or during a sprint finish in a race.

> Plyometric training involves exercises such as jumping, to improve power in the legs. Power is an important component of fitness in cycling, as it is used to pedal forcefully and quickly, helping a cyclist to maintain a high speed. It also allows a cyclist to accelerate quickly, so they can overtake other riders in a race.

This shows knowledge of plyometric training and applies it to the cyclist's performance.

This paragraph outlines the disadvantages of plyometric training for a cyclist.

> However, plyometric training alone is not the most suitable training method for a cyclist, as it does not provide practice of sport-specific actions, such as pedalling technique.

This bit shows that the training methods are being evaluated by making a judgement about their usefulness.

> In conclusion, a combination of continuous and plyometric training would be very useful for a cyclist wishing to improve their performance. Using both training methods would help to improve a cyclist's muscular endurance, cardiovascular fitness and power, all of which would lead to improved cycling performance. However, a cyclist wishing to improve their performance further might also use interval training, which would improve their ability to exercise at high intensities.

You could really show off by bringing a different training method into your conclusion.

Total for Question 15 = 9 marks

Answers

Section One — Anatomy and Physiology

Page 1 — The Skeletal System
Q1 E.g. Bones store minerals like calcium and phosphorus, which help maintain bone strength *[1 mark]*. Strong bones are essential for performance in physical activity and sport, as they reduce the chance of the bones becoming broken through the stress placed on them during exercise *[1 mark]*.

You could also say that these minerals also enable muscle contractions, which allow someone taking part in physical activity to perform the necessary sports movements.

Page 2 — The Skeletal System
Q1 The tibia and fibula *[1 mark for each]*

Page 3 — The Skeletal System
Q1 Ball and socket *[1 mark]*

Page 4 — The Skeletal System
Q1 E.g. During a netball pass, flexion at the elbow occurs in order to bring the ball backwards towards the player *[1 mark]*. Next, extension at the elbow occurs, straightening the arm and propelling the ball forward towards the target *[1 mark]*.

Q2 Cartilage covers the ends of bones that meet at joints *[1 mark]*, acting as a cushion between them *[1 mark]*. This allows a performer to use their joints for movement during sport without damage to the bones as they rub against each other *[1 mark]*.

Page 6 — The Muscular System
Q1 The hip flexors *[1 mark]*

When kicking a football, the hip flexors allow flexion at the hip so the entire leg swings forward.

Page 7 — The Muscular System
Q1 The quadriceps *[1 mark]*

During the lowering phase of a squat, the quadriceps contracts eccentrically at the knee to control how quickly you move towards the ground.

Q2 **A** Type I *[1 mark]*

Type I muscle fibres are better suited to long periods of exercise than other muscle fibre types.

Page 8 — The Cardiovascular System
Q1 E.g. The pulmonary artery carries deoxygenated blood *[1 mark]* to the lungs, where it becomes oxygenated *[1 mark]*. This is essential for physical activity and sport as this oxygenated blood can then be delivered to the muscles *[1 mark]* to provide the oxygen needed for exercise *[1 mark]*.

Page 9 — The Cardiovascular System
Q1 E.g. Capillaries have very thin walls *[1 mark]* which allow substances to pass through them easily *[1 mark]*. This means that oxygen can quickly be transferred from the capillaries to the muscles to release the energy needed for physical activity *[1 mark]*.

You could also say that the thin walls let carbon dioxide pass easily from the muscles back to the capillaries. Or you could have mentioned a different characteristic of capillaries, like their narrow diameters, and how this gives more time for oxygen and carbon dioxide to be exchanged with the muscles.

Page 10 — The Respiratory System
Q1 E.g. Deoxygenated blood becomes oxygenated through gas exchange between the capillaries containing the deoxygenated blood and the alveoli containing oxygen *[1 mark]*. Oxygen diffuses from an area of higher concentration (the alveoli) *[1 mark]* to an area of lower concentration (the deoxygenated blood) *[1 mark]*.

Page 11 — The Respiratory System
Q1 E.g. An athlete with a high vital capacity can breathe in a large amount of oxygen and can breathe out a large amount of carbon dioxide *[1 mark]*. This is beneficial to an athlete because it means that more oxygen can be delivered to the muscles to allow them to move during physical activity *[1 mark]*. It also means that more carbon dioxide can be carried away from the muscles and out of the body *[1 mark]*.

Page 12 — Spirometers
Q1 The lung volume shown at 'A' is tidal volume, which increases during exercise *[1 mark]*. This would be shown by larger 'peaks' on the spirometer trace *[1 mark]*.

Page 13 — Aerobic and Anaerobic Exercise
Q1 E.g. A 100 metre sprint would be an anaerobic activity because it is a high intensity and short duration event *[1 mark]*. In the time taken to run 100 metres, the body systems would be unable to deliver oxygen quickly enough for the muscles to use aerobic respiration *[1 mark]*, so the muscles would release energy without oxygen *[1 mark]*.

Page 14 — Short-Term Effects of Exercise
Q1 E.g. A footballer experiencing muscle fatigue may be unable to sprint with the ball. This could make them less likely to score a goal *[1 mark]*.

Page 15 — Short-Term Effects of Exercise
Q1 During exercise, the **heart rate** *[1 mark]* and stroke volume increase. This leads to an increase in the **cardiac** *[1 mark]* output so more oxygenated **blood** *[1 mark]* is delivered to the muscles.

Answers

Q2 Vasoconstriction is the narrowing of blood vessels *[1 mark]*. This would occur in the stomach during exercise as part of the process known as 'vascular shunting' in order to reduce the amount of blood being delivered to the stomach *[1 mark]*. This would leave more blood, and therefore more oxygen, available for the working muscles, where it would be used to release the extra energy needed for exercise *[1 mark]*.

Page 16 — Short-Term Effects of Exercise

Q1 a) 63 cm³ *[1 mark]*
   b) 141 cm³ *[1 mark]*
   Stroke volume increases during exercise and slowly returns to normal after exercise has stopped. So the lowest value in the table must have been recorded before exercise started, and the highest must have been during exercise.

Page 17 — Long-Term Effects of Exercise

Q1 E.g. Muscle hypertrophy means an increase in muscle thickness *[1 mark]*. This would benefit a performer participating in weightlifting because it would increase their strength *[1 mark]*, meaning they would be able to lift heavier weights *[1 mark]*.

Section Two — Movement Analysis

Page 19 — Lever Systems

Q1 First class *[1 mark]*
   When the ball is released during a football throw-in, the elbow is moving from flexion to extension, which uses a first class lever.

Page 20 — Planes and Axes of Movement

Q1 Frontal plane *[1 mark]* and sagittal axis *[1 mark]* (or frontal axis if you're doing the OCR course)
   A star jump involves abduction and adduction of the arms and legs. These movements use the frontal plane and sagittal axis.

Section Three — Physical Training

Page 22 — Health and Fitness

Q1 E.g. An athlete could train too much *[1 mark]*. This might give them a high level of fitness, but cause them to get injured *[1 mark]*.

Page 23 — Components of Fitness

Q1 E.g. Muscular endurance allows you to repeatedly use voluntary muscles without getting tired *[1 mark]*. A long-distance cyclist uses the same leg muscles over a long period of time *[1 mark]*, so muscular endurance is very important in preventing fatigue in the later stages of a race and in helping the cyclist to sprint at the end *[1 mark]*.
   Any reasonable application of muscular endurance to a cycling race will get you the third mark here.

Page 24 — Components of Fitness

Q1 E.g. Flexibility will help the swimmer avoid injury, meaning they can train more, which will help them perform better *[1 mark]*.
   Flexibility will help the swimmer achieve longer/more efficient strokes *[1 mark]*.

Page 25 — Components of Fitness

Q1 E.g. Coordination is the ability to use two or more parts of the body together, efficiently and accurately *[1 mark]*.
   Make sure your definition talks about using two or more parts of the body, and you'll get the mark.
   E.g. A boxer needs good hand-eye coordination to be able to throw a punch accurately *[1 mark]*.
   Any example of using two or more body parts together in boxing is okay for the second mark.

Page 26 — Components of Fitness

Q1 E.g. A rugby player uses power to kick the ball a long way *[1 mark]* and to tackle another player to the ground *[1 mark]*.
   Remember that power is a combination of strength and speed. There are lots of other examples — e.g. jumping for the ball or sprinting for the try line.

Page 27 — Fitness Testing

Q1 Any two from: e.g.
   To identify your strengths and weaknesses / to monitor your progress / to evaluate how successful your training programme is / to get a starting (baseline) level of fitness / so you can compare your fitness with national averages *[1 mark for each]*.

Page 28 — Fitness Testing

Q1 Strength (or 'muscular strength') *[1 mark]*

Page 29 — Fitness Testing

Q1 E.g. Stand on your best leg with your hands on your hips and your other foot touching your knee. Then stand on your toes and time how long you can hold the position in seconds. The test is over if you move your hands from your hips, your heel touches the floor, or you move your non-standing leg. You take the best of three times in seconds to measure balance.
   [2 marks available in total]
   Even though this question is only worth two marks, it's worth describing the test in plenty of detail to make sure that you get both marks.

Page 30 — Fitness Testing

Q1 E.g. The sit and reach test measures flexibility in the lower hamstrings and back *[1 mark]*. Flexibility of the hamstrings and back affect how high a kickboxer can kick, so the sit and reach test could be a suitable test *[1 mark]*. However, the action involved in the sit and reach test is nothing like the action involved in kicking (it's not a sport-specific test), so the results may be misleading *[1 mark]*.

Page 31 — Fitness Testing

Q1 C Average *[1 mark]*
   Sarah's female and her time of 5.7 s falls between 5.60 s and 5.89 s — it's in the 'Average' column.

Page 32 — Principles of Training

Q1 E.g. A rower could train using a rowing machine *[1 mark]*, as this would work the same muscles as they use in their sport *[1 mark]*.

Answers

Page 33 — Principles of Training
Q1 E.g. Overtraining means not allowing enough time between training sessions for your body to recover *[1 mark]*. It can lead to injury, which will stop you training and lead to a decrease in fitness *[1 mark]*.

Page 34 — Training Target Zones
Q1 220 − 35 = 185 *[1 mark]*
185 × 0.8 *[1 mark]* = 148 bpm *[1 mark]*

The first mark is for finding the maximum heart rate (220 − age). The second mark is for using the right decimal for the threshold. And the last mark is for getting the maths right and getting the correct answer.

Page 35 — Training Methods
Q1 E.g. Continuous training is good aerobic training *[1 mark]*. This means it is well suited to aerobic endurance activities like marathon running *[1 mark]*. However, continuous training does not improve anaerobic fitness *[1 mark]*, so is not well suited to anaerobic activities like sprinting *[1 mark]*.

Page 36 — Training Methods
Q1 E.g. For strength training, an athlete needs to use a high weight and do a low number of reps *[1 mark]*. They can overload by gradually increasing the weight used *[1 mark]*.

If you're doing the AQA course, you will need to make sure you say that a high weight is above 70% of your one rep max.

Page 37 — Training Methods
Q1 E.g. Plyometric training increases power *[1 mark]*, which would help the basketball player to jump higher *[1 mark]*, increasing their ability to make interceptions *[1 mark]*.

One mark is for saying plyometric training improves power. One mark is for identifying an action that power helps with — e.g. jumping, sprinting, shooting. And one mark is for linking this to a specific basketball skill — e.g. lay-ups are easier when you can jump higher / sprinting faster allows you to get past opponents / a more powerful shot will help you to score three-point shots.

Page 38 — Training Methods
Q1 E.g. In pre-season training, performers need to improve the specific components of fitness they will need to compete *[1 mark]*. A high jumper could use plyometric training to improve their power, through exercises such as bounding or depth jumps *[1 mark]*. A high jumper needs power to achieve as much height on take-off as possible *[1 mark]*.

Page 39 — Preventing Injuries
Q1 E.g. A rugby referee can enforce the rules, so players are less likely to be injured through bad tackles *[1 mark]*.

Page 40 — Preventing Injuries
Q1 *This mark scheme gives examples of some points you might have made in your answer, and how many marks you'd get for making those points. You can still get full marks if you haven't written every individual point below, as long as the points you've made are detailed enough.*

You will get up to three marks for showing knowledge and understanding of a warm-up, for example:
- A warm-up includes light aerobic exercise to gradually increase your pulse rate.
- A warm-up includes stretching the muscles that will be used in the activity.
- A warm-up can include practice actions to prepare the muscles that will be used during the activity.

You will get up to six marks if you also include examples of how the warm-up can help prevent injuries in hockey, for example:
- Practising passing the ball in the warm-up helps prepare the shoulder and arm muscles for passing during the hockey match, so they're warm and less likely to get injured.
- Stretching the leg muscles will help to improve their flexibility, which will help the player to avoid injury when they lunge to reach the ball.
- The light exercise eases the player's body into more intense exercise, which helps them to avoid injury when they need to sprint to outrun other players during the hockey match.

You will get up to nine marks if you also evaluate the importance of a warm-up in preventing injury. You can include comparisons with other methods of preventing injury in a hockey match. For example:
- A warm-up is necessary for a hockey player to avoid injury, because stretching and practice actions help prepare the player's muscles for the strenuous actions they'll perform in the match, like lunging for the ball or sprinting.
- However, it is also important to play by the rules to avoid injury, as foul play using a hockey stick can lead to serious injuries. Protective equipment, such as gumshields and shinpads, is also necessary to prevent injuries.
- In conclusion, a warm-up is absolutely vital before a hockey match to help prevent injury. However a warm-up alone is not sufficient to prevent all types of injury, so other measures must also be taken.
[9 marks available in total]

Page 41 — Injuries and Treatment
Q1 Ligaments (or 'a ligament') *[1 mark]*

Sprains are joint injuries where the ligament has been stretched or torn.

Page 42 — Injuries and Treatment
Q1 You can use the RICE method to treat a sprain *[1 mark]*. The injured person should stop and rest, apply ice and a bandage to their ankle and elevate it above their heart *[1 mark]*.

It's not enough to just write RICE here — make sure you apply it to the specific injury to get 2 marks.

Page 43 — Performance-Enhancing Drugs
Q1 E.g. Beta blockers might benefit an archer because they have a calming effect and steady shaking hands *[1 mark]*, which will help the archer keep steady as they take aim and shoot *[1 mark]*.

There are a few different performance-enhancing drugs that might improve an archer's performance. The first mark comes from explaining what the drug does. And the second mark comes from applying that effect to archery.

Answers

Section Four — Health, Fitness and Well-being

Page 45 — Health, Fitness and Well-being

Q1 Either:
You are far more at risk of type-2 diabetes when you are overweight *[1 mark]*.
Exercise helps you to maintain a healthy weight, so helps prevent type-2 diabetes. *[1 mark]*.
Or:
Exercise helps to improve your insulin sensitivity *[1 mark]*.
This means you are less likely to become insulin-resistant, so are less likely to get type-2 diabetes. *[1 mark]*.

Page 46 — Health, Fitness and Well-being

Q1 Any two from: e.g.
Exercise relieves stress/tension / it can help you learn to cope with pressure/manage emotions / it can increase self-esteem and confidence / it can increase your levels of endorphins, which makes you feel good / gains in physical health can help to improve your body-image *[1 mark for each]*.

You need to give two benefits for two marks — so you don't need to go into any depth.

Page 47 — Lifestyle Choices

Q1 E.g. Chemicals in the smoke damage cilia *[1 mark]*.
This increases the risk of infection of the airways *[1 mark]*, which can lead to bronchitis *[1 mark]*.

There are lots of different answers you can give here — just make sure that you say enough to get three marks. You get one mark for naming the health problem, one for explaining the damage that smoking causes and one for saying how that damage causes the disease.

Page 48 — Sedentary Lifestyle

Q1 Any two from: e.g.
Osteoporosis / depression / high blood pressure / coronary heart disease / diabetes *[1 mark for each]*.

Page 49 — Diet and Nutrition
Q1 Carbohydrates *[1 mark]*

Page 50 — Diet and Nutrition

Q1 E.g. Exercise causes your body temperature to rise *[1 mark]*. If your temperature rises high enough, then you will lose water through sweat. This could cause dehydration *[1 mark]*.

You also lose water through breathing. Exercise makes you breathe more frequently and heavily, so this could also dehydrate you.

Page 51 — Diet, Nutrition and Performance

Q1 The triathlete would benefit more from carbohydrate loading *[1 mark]*. This is because the triathlon is an endurance event, so the triathlete's muscles will need a large amount of stored energy to last a long time *[1 mark]*. Weightlifting is a short duration event, so the weightlifter doesn't need as much stored energy *[1 mark]*.

Page 52 — Somatotypes

Q1 E.g. Ectomorphs are well suited to being long-distance runners *[1 mark]*, because being light and having long legs means they can run very efficiently *[1 mark]*.

Page 53 — Optimum Weight

Q1 Any two from: e.g.
They could have different bone structures / different muscle girths / compete in different types of events that have different weight requirements *[1 mark for each]*.

Section Five — Sport Psychology

Page 55 — Learning Skills

Q1 E.g. An efficient technique is important for a marathon runner because the more efficient their technique, the less energy they will use *[1 mark]*. Therefore, an efficient technique would help them to run for the duration of a marathon without becoming too tired to continue *[1 mark]*.

You could also say that an efficient running technique would use less time, allowing a runner to complete a marathon more quickly.

Page 56 — Skills and Practice

Q1 E.g. Catching a cricket ball would be a relatively open skill because of the need for a performer to react to external factors *[1 mark]*, for example, by adjusting their position on the pitch depending on where the ball is hit *[1 mark]*. However, it is not a completely open skill, as some elements are unaffected by external factors. For example, once in the correct position on the pitch, a performer would usually make the same shape with their hands to catch the ball *[1 mark]*.

Page 57 — Goal Setting

Q1 E.g. This goal does not apply the 'measurable' principle *[1 mark]*. It is not measurable because it does not say how much faster the athlete would like to run *[1 mark]*.

You could also say that the goal doesn't apply the 'specific' principle for the same reason.

Page 58 — Guidance and Feedback

Q1 This mark scheme gives examples of some points you might have made in your answer, and how many marks you'd get for making those points. You can still get full marks if you haven't written every individual point below, as long as the points you've made are detailed enough.

You will get up to three marks for showing knowledge and understanding of the different types of guidance, for example:
- Verbal guidance includes instructions given in words.
- Verbal guidance involves a coach explaining how to perform a skill.
- Manual guidance involves a coach moving the performer's body through a technique.

You will get up to six marks if you also apply your knowledge of guidance to a beginner in golf, for example:
- Verbal guidance could include the coach telling the learner how to position their legs before swinging the club.

Answers

- Manual guidance could include the coach moving the learner's arms through a golf swing.
- Verbal and manual guidance could be used at the same time. For example, the coach could manually position the learner's hands on the club, while explaining how they should be positioned.

You will get up to nine marks if you also evaluate which guidance type would be best for use with a beginner golfer. For example:

- Manual guidance can be useful for beginners as it gives them the feel of the correct technique. However, it can lead to the learner relying on it.
- Verbal guidance alone may be confusing for a beginner, as they may be unable to picture how a technique should feel due to their limited experience in golf.
- In conclusion, it would be best to combine verbal and manual guidance to improve a beginner's performance in golf. This would allow the learner to experience how golfing techniques feel while having them explained by the coach, to make sure they understand them.

[9 marks available in total]

Page 59 — Using Feedback

Q1 E.g. Praise is an example of positive feedback *[1 mark]*. This would teach the beginner that they should continue to use this stance on the snowboard *[1 mark]*, improving their future performance *[1 mark]*.

You could also say that this is extrinsic feedback, which is useful for beginners as they lack the knowledge needed to assess their own performance.

Page 60 — Mental Preparation

Q1 E.g. A football player may feel under a lot of pressure before taking a penalty, so could use mental rehearsal to help improve their confidence *[1 mark]*.

Page 61 — Emotion and Personality

Q1 **C** A medal *[1 mark]*

A medal is tangible because you can actually hold it and touch it. It's extrinsic because you'd get it from another person, not from yourself.

Section Six — Sport, Society and Culture

Page 63 — Influences on Participation

Q1 E.g. The attitudes your friends have about taking part in physical activity could influence your attitude *[1 mark]*. If they don't like sport, this could put pressure on you to also not take part in sport *[1 mark]*.

Page 64 — Influences on Participation

Q1 E.g. Local facilities might not provide many opportunities for disabled people to play sports, so you might be unable to participate *[1 mark]*.

Page 65 — Influences on Participation

Q1 Any two from: e.g. Students could be allowed to choose from a range of activities / the school could invest in new facilities, equipment or changing rooms / the school could offer non-competitive options in PE / the school could bring in outside agencies to help with coaching and development *[1 mark for each]*.

Page 66 — Influences on Participation

Q1 **B** Cycling *[1 mark]*

Page 67 — Commercialisation of Sport

Q1 E.g. Media coverage of sports creates role models *[1 mark]*. This can inspire people watching the sport to participate *[1 mark]*. Media coverage of a sport allows it to reach a much larger audience *[1 mark]*. This means that more people will become aware of the sport and learn about it, which may encourage them to take it up *[1 mark]*.

With each point, make sure you say enough to get two marks by saying how the media's coverage of sport encourages people to take part.

Page 68 — Commercialisation of Sport

Q1 E.g. Sponsorship by a fast-food company would have a positive impact because it would give the team more money *[1 mark]*. This would allow them to buy more

equipment or improve facilities *[1 mark]*, helping the team to improve their performance *[1 mark]*. However, by being promoted by the football team, the fast-food company could gain a false image of health *[1 mark]*. As it is an under-12's team, the young players and supporters may be influenced to eat more fast food *[1 mark]*, which could lead to an increased risk of obesity *[1 mark]*.

You get three marks for your 'positive' answer and three marks for your 'negative' answer. To get all three marks in each case you need to explain what effect the sponsorship will have, and why that is good or bad.

Page 69 — Technology in Sport

Q1 This mark scheme gives examples of some points you might have made in your answer, and how many marks you'd get for making those points. You can still get full marks if you haven't written every individual point below, as long as the points you've made are detailed enough.

You will get up to three marks for showing knowledge and understanding of technology in sport, for example:

- New materials can be used to make sportspeople's equipment and clothing more effective.
- Video recordings and training software can help coaches analyse performers' movement.
- Systems like Hawk-Eye have been introduced to help officials.

You will get up to six marks if you also give examples of technology being used in sport with a positive or negative effect, for example:

- Using new materials to make swimming costumes has improved the performances of swimmers.
- Using software to analyse an athlete's movement in the 100 m sprint allows the athlete and their coach to fine-tune their technique.
- Some umpires in cricket are concerned that by using technology to support their decisions, this undermines their authority on the pitch, which could lead to players not respecting their decisions.

You will get up to nine marks if you also weigh up the positives and the negatives, for example:

Answers

- Use of analysis technology in training can lead to new levels of achievement in sport. However, this technology is expensive, so people who can't afford it might not be able to compete on a level playing field with those with more money.
- Using technology to support officials makes sport fairer as it helps ensure correct decisions are made. As long as these technologies don't lead to long breaks in play, they improve the sport for spectators, officials and players.
- Better swimming costumes have helped swimmers set new world records, which has made the sport very exciting. However, it does run the risk of making swimming more about the technology involved in the costume, and less about the ability of the swimmers themselves.
[9 marks available in total]

Page 70 — Sporting Behaviour

Q1 E.g. Deviance is where a participant in a sport breaks the laws of the game *[1 mark]*, whereas gamesmanship only involves bending the rules, without actually breaking them *[1 mark]*.

Page 71 — Spectator Behaviour

Q1 Any two from: e.g. Rivalries between fans / media hyping up the game so people take it too seriously / drinking or drug taking amongst fans / frustration with the way the game is going or decisions made by officials / a gang culture meaning fans feel less responsible for their actions / peer pressure from other supporters to join in rowdy and violent behaviour *[1 mark for each]*.

Section Seven — Using Data

Page 73 — Using Data

Q1 Any one from: e.g. Data from fitness tests can be used to monitor a performer's improvements in training / you can measure individual aspects of a performance (like goals scored) to track improvement / you can measure heart rate to make sure the performer is training at the correct intensity *[1 mark]*.

Page 74 — Using Data

Q1 Sarah *[1 mark]*

Sarah had an increase of 6, from 2 tackles to 8. Jenny only increased by 3, from 3 tackles to 6.

Page 75 — Using Data

Q1 B 66 bpm *[1 mark]*

Page 76 — Using Data

Q1 2011 *[1 mark]*

Page 77 — Using Data

Q1 No, Nadège's average speed decreased between weeks 6 and 7 *[1 mark]*.

Glossary

abduction	Movement <u>away</u> from an imaginary <u>centre line</u> through the body.
ability	A person's set of <u>characteristics</u> that control their <u>potential</u> to <u>learn a skill</u>.
adduction	Movement <u>towards</u> an imaginary <u>centre line</u> through the body.
aerobic respiration	When the body releases <u>energy</u> using <u>glucose</u> and <u>oxygen</u>. <u>Carbon dioxide</u> and <u>water</u> are produced as by-products (waste).
agility	The <u>ability</u> to change <u>body position</u> or <u>direction</u> quickly and with control.
alveoli	Small <u>air bags</u> in the <u>lungs</u> where gases are exchanged.
anaerobic respiration	When the body doesn't have <u>enough oxygen</u> to release energy aerobically, so it just uses <u>glucose</u>. <u>Lactic acid</u> is produced as a by-product (waste).
antagonistic muscle pair	A pair of muscles that work <u>together</u> to bring about movement. As one muscle <u>contracts</u> (the <u>agonist</u> or <u>prime mover</u>) the other <u>relaxes</u> (the <u>antagonist</u>).
anticipatory rise	When heart rate <u>increases before exercise</u> has started.
arousal	A person's level of mental and physical <u>alertness</u>.
ATP-PC	The <u>anaerobic energy system</u> used in the muscles during the <u>first few seconds</u> of exercise.
axis of movement	An <u>imaginary line</u> that the body or a body part can <u>move around</u>.
balance	The ability to keep the body's <u>centre of mass</u> over a <u>base of support</u>.
balanced diet	The best <u>ratio</u> of <u>nutrients</u> to match your <u>lifestyle</u>.
basic skill	A <u>simple</u> skill which doesn't need much concentration to do, e.g. running.
blood cell	A component of <u>blood</u>. There are <u>red blood cells</u> (which carry oxygen and carbon dioxide) and <u>white blood cells</u> (which fight disease).
blood pressure	How <u>strongly</u> the blood presses against the walls of <u>blood vessels</u>.
blood vessel	Part of the cardiovascular system that <u>transports blood</u> around the body. The three main types are <u>arteries</u>, <u>veins</u> and <u>capillaries</u>.
body composition	The <u>percentage</u> of body <u>weight</u> made up by <u>fat</u>, <u>muscle</u> and <u>bone</u>.
body mass index (BMI)	A <u>score</u> used to determine whether a person is underweight, overweight, obese or of a normal weight. It's calculated using their <u>height</u> and <u>weight</u>.
breathing rate	The <u>number of breaths</u> taken <u>each minute</u>.
calorie	A <u>unit</u> used to measure the amount of <u>energy in food</u>. It's often shortened to <u>Kcal</u>.
cardiac output	The <u>volume of blood</u> pumped by each ventricle in the heart per minute.
cardio-respiratory system	The combination of the <u>cardiovascular</u> and <u>respiratory</u> systems working together to get <u>oxygen</u> into the body tissues and <u>carbon dioxide</u> out of them.
cardiovascular endurance/fitness	The ability of the <u>heart</u> and <u>lungs</u> to supply <u>oxygen</u> to the <u>muscles</u>, so that the whole body can be <u>exercised</u> for a <u>long time</u>. It can also be called aerobic endurance, aerobic power or stamina.
cardiovascular system	The <u>organs</u> responsible for <u>circulating blood</u> around the body.
circumduction	Movement of a limb, hand or foot in a <u>circular motion</u>.
closed skill	A skill performed in a <u>predictable environment</u> — it's not affected by external factors.

Glossary

commercialisation	The commercialisation of sport means the <u>transformation</u> of sport into something people can make <u>money</u> from, e.g. through <u>sponsorship</u>.
complex skill	A skill which needs lots of <u>concentration</u> to do, e.g. a volley in football.
concentric contraction	A type of muscle contraction where a muscle contracts and <u>shortens</u>.
connective tissue	Body tissue that <u>holds</u> other body tissues (e.g. muscles and bones) <u>together</u>. Cartilage, ligaments and tendons are types of connective tissue.
contract to compete	An <u>unwritten agreement</u> between competitors to <u>respect</u> the '<u>spirit of the game</u>'.
cool-down	<u>Light exercise</u> and <u>stretching</u> done <u>after exercise</u> to return your body to normal.
coordination	The ability to use <u>two or more</u> parts of the body <u>together</u>, efficiently and accurately.
coronary heart disease	When <u>fatty deposits</u> build up in the <u>arteries</u> around the heart, which <u>restrict</u> the flow of <u>blood</u>.
data	<u>Information</u> — in <u>words</u> or <u>numbers</u>. Data can be <u>quantitative</u> (numbers) or <u>qualitative</u> (words).
delayed onset of muscle soreness (DOMS)	<u>Soreness</u> in the muscles in the <u>days after exercise</u>.
deviance	Behaviour that goes <u>against</u> the <u>moral values</u> or <u>laws</u> of the sport.
diffusion	The process of <u>substances</u> (e.g. oxygen) <u>moving</u> from a place where there is a <u>higher concentration</u> to a place where there is a <u>lower concentration</u>.
dorsi-flexion	<u>Flexion</u> at the <u>ankle</u> by lifting the toes.
eccentric contraction	A type of muscle contraction where a muscle contracts and <u>lengthens</u>.
effort arm	The <u>distance</u> between the <u>fulcrum</u> and the <u>effort</u> in a lever system.
exercise	A form of physical activity done to <u>maintain</u> or <u>improve health</u> and/or <u>fitness</u>.
expiratory reserve volume (ERV)	The amount of <u>extra air</u> that can be <u>breathed out</u> after breathing out normally.
extension	<u>Opening a joint</u>, e.g. straightening the leg at the knee.
externally-paced skill	A skill that starts because of <u>external factors</u> which also <u>control the pace</u> of the skill.
feedback	<u>Information</u> received <u>about a performance</u> either during it (<u>concurrent</u> feedback) or after it (<u>terminal</u> feedback). It can be <u>intrinsic</u> (from yourself) or <u>extrinsic</u> (from other sources).
fine skill	A skill using <u>small muscle groups</u> for <u>precise</u> movements requiring <u>accuracy</u> and <u>coordination</u>.
fitness	The ability to meet the <u>demands</u> of the <u>environment</u>.
flexibility	The amount of <u>movement</u> possible at a <u>joint</u>.
flexion	<u>Closing a joint</u>, e.g. bending the arm at the elbow.
gamesmanship	Gaining an <u>advantage</u> by using tactics that <u>seem unfair</u>, but aren't against the rules.
gross skill	A skill involving <u>powerful movements</u> performed by <u>large muscle groups</u>.
guidance	<u>Information</u> or <u>help</u> in learning a skill. Guidance can be visual, verbal, manual or mechanical.
health	A state of complete <u>physical</u>, <u>mental</u> and <u>social well-being</u> and not merely the absence of disease or infirmity.

Glossary

heart rate	The number of times your heart beats in one minute. It is measured in beats per minute (bpm).
high organisation skill	A skill which can't easily be broken down into different parts that can be practised separately, because the parts of the skill are closely linked. E.g. a cartwheel.
hooliganism	Rowdy, aggressive and sometimes violent behaviour of fans and spectators of sport.
hydration	Having the right amount of water for the body to function properly. If you have too little water, you're dehydrated.
inspiratory reserve volume (IRV)	The amount of extra air that can be breathed in after breathing in normally.
isometric contraction	When a muscle stays the same length as it contracts.
isotonic contraction	When a muscle changes length as it contracts.
joint type	The main types of joint are ball and socket, hinge, condyloid and pivot. Each type allows a different range of movement.
lactic acid	A waste product produced during anaerobic respiration, making the muscles feel tired (fatigued).
lever system	A system that allows the body's muscles to move the bones in the skeleton. A lever system can be first, second or third class, and is made up of a lever arm, effort, fulcrum and load.
low organisation skill	A skill which can easily be broken down into different parts that can be practised separately. E.g. the front crawl stroke in swimming.
mechanical advantage	When a lever can move a large load with a small amount of effort from the muscles.
mechanical disadvantage	When a lever requires a large effort from the muscles to move a small load.
the media	Organisations involved in mass communication — e.g. through television, radio, newspapers and the Internet.
minute ventilation	The volume of air breathed in or out in one minute. It can also be called 'minute volume'.
muscle fibre	One of the fibres that make up the muscles in the body. There are three main types: type I, type IIA and type IIX. Each type is suited to a different intensity of exercise.
muscular endurance	The ability to repeatedly use the muscles over a long time, without getting tired.
musculo-skeletal system	The combination of the muscular and skeletal systems working together to allow movement.
obesity	Having a lot more body fat than you should.
open skill	A skill performed in a changing environment, where a performer has to react and adapt to external factors.
optimum weight	Roughly what you should weigh for good health, based on your gender, height, bone structure and muscle girth. It can also be affected by the kind of activity or sport you do.
overload	Working your body harder to increase fitness levels over time.
PEP	Personal Exercise Programme. A training programme that's designed to suit a specific person and improve their health, fitness or performance.
performance	How well a task is completed.
plane of movement	An imaginary flat surface used to describe the direction of a movement. The body or a body part moves in a plane. There are three planes you need to know: sagittal, transverse and frontal.
plantar-flexion	Extension at the ankle by pointing the toes.

Glossary

power	A combination of <u>speed</u> and <u>strength</u>.
practice	When a <u>skill is repeated</u> to improve it. The types of practice are massed, distributed, fixed, variable, whole and part.
reaction time	The time taken to <u>move</u> in <u>response</u> to a stimulus.
residual volume	The amount of <u>air left</u> in the lungs after the <u>most possible</u> air has been <u>breathed out</u>.
resistance/load arm	The <u>distance</u> between the <u>fulcrum</u> and the <u>load</u> in a lever system.
respiratory system	The <u>organs</u> in the body used for <u>breathing</u>.
rotation	Movement of the body or a body part in a <u>clockwise</u> or <u>anticlockwise</u> motion.
sedentary lifestyle	A lifestyle where there is <u>little</u>, <u>irregular</u> or <u>no physical activity</u>.
self-paced skill	A skill that <u>starts</u> when a <u>performer decides</u> to start it. The performer also controls the <u>pace</u> of the skill.
SMART	The <u>five principles of goal setting</u>.
socio-economic group	A way of grouping people based on their <u>job</u>, how much <u>money</u> they have and <u>where they live</u>, e.g. 'working class' is a socio-economic group.
somatotype	A person's <u>body type</u> based on their <u>body shape</u> and the amount of <u>muscle</u> and <u>fat</u> they have. The main somatotypes are <u>endomorph</u>, <u>mesomorph</u> and <u>ectomorph</u>.
speed	The <u>rate</u> at which someone is able to <u>move</u>, or to <u>cover</u> a <u>distance</u> in a given amount of <u>time</u>.
spirometer trace	A <u>graph</u> produced by a spirometer machine which can be used to measure <u>lung volumes</u>.
sponsorship	When a <u>company</u> pays to associate their <u>name</u> with some part of a <u>sport</u>, including individual <u>sportspeople</u>. It's usually done to make <u>money</u>.
sportsmanship	Being <u>honest</u>, sticking to the <u>rules</u> and treating your opponents with <u>respect</u>.
stage of learning	How <u>experienced</u> someone is at performing a skill. The stages are cognitive, associative and autonomous.
strength	The amount of <u>force</u> that a <u>muscle</u> or <u>muscle group</u> can apply against a <u>resistance</u>. It can be broken down into <u>different types</u>: maximal, static, explosive and dynamic.
stroke volume	The <u>volume of blood</u> pumped with each <u>heartbeat</u> by each ventricle in the heart.
synovial joint	Where two or more <u>bones</u> are <u>joined together</u> in a joint capsule containing synovial fluid.
tidal volume	The <u>amount of air</u> that is breathed in or out in <u>one breath</u>.
training season	One of the <u>three parts</u> of the <u>year</u> with different training aims depending on whether it's <u>before</u>, <u>during</u> or <u>after</u> the period when sport competition takes place.
trend	When a graph is generally going <u>up</u> or <u>down</u> over time.
vertebral column	The bones (<u>vertebrae</u>) making up the spine/spinal column. The vertebral column has five regions: cervical, thoracic, lumbar, the sacrum and the coccyx.
vital capacity	The <u>most air</u> you can possibly <u>breathe in</u> after breathing out the largest volume of air possible.
warm-up	<u>Preparing</u> your body for <u>exercise</u>. It's made up of <u>three</u> main phases: light exercise, stretching and practice actions.

Index

Index